Dedication

This book is dedicated to you. You are my co-author.

Just like in competition, you will never unlock your own excellence if you are competing against an unworthy opponent. This is a similar partnership. As you read, you'll realize this book is not complete. It requires your reflection and vulnerable truth to make it whole and fulfill its purpose. You are the protagonist and hero of this story. I simply provide prompts, questions, and space to help you write—or maybe even rewrite—your destiny.

Similar to the law of gravity, there are fundamental "laws of success." These truths have never changed and have been practiced for centuries. I will share these learnings with you. Study these truths, become a practitioner of these laws, and you will become limitless.

I'm excited to be your guide in this journey of self-discovery. If used correctly, this book has the power to radically change the trajectory of your life and give you the most powerful resource there is: a quiet mind.

"Do not conform to the patterns of this world, but be transformed by the renewing of your mind."
–Romans 12:2

TABLE OF CONTENTS

INTRODUCTION
origin story: the tantrum

While looking at me in disgust, my wife, Kendra, thought to herself, *Seriously, is this who I married?*

Kendra shared with me this honest and chilling fact recently, while enjoying our Saturday morning donuts and Starbucks (if you are wondering, I'm drinking an iced vanilla latte and slamming a chocolate ring donut... my favorite).

Huddled over our kitchen island, we were reflecting on how far we both have grown over the years. She brought up the now infamous "tantrum." Looking back, the event she described is completely comical and laughable, but in the moment, it surely wasn't. The day she referred to was in March of 2014—the day everything changed.

Looking back, I don't blame her. Let me take you to that moment, a time that was one of the lowest points in my life, one in which my wife actually questioned her judgment in choosing me as her life partner.

It was a crisp Pacific Northwest spring afternoon, and we were just outside our house along a gravel trail. This path was nestled near a pond leading into the woods filled with endless evergreen trees. Walking on the trail, I was throwing a tantrum just like a 3-year-old who was told they couldn't watch another episode of Peppa Pig before bedtime. I had my hands in two fists with a scowl that would make the Grinch cringe. I was pissed off—so pissed I actually stomped my feet several times kicking up rocks and dust.

"*I missed the interview!*" I yelled while throwing my arms up and watching my warm breath fill the chilled air with each word.

While pushing our almost 2-year-old son and newborn daughter in a stroller, Kendra asked me with a perplexed look, "What the hell happened? And why are you acting like a baby?" *Kendra has a gift for cutting straight to the point.*

"I got off at baggage claim," I mumbled with my teeth clenched and smoke coming out of my ears.

Let me interrupt myself to ask you two questions:
Have you ever made an embarrassing, boneheaded mistake?
Have you ever hit a serious rough patch in life?

Well, I was living in both of those realities that day.

First, here's my dumb mistake. I had planned on meeting with a district manager of a Fortune 500 medical device company at the SeaTac Airport food court. It was supposed to be a quick, last-minute interview for a peripheral vascular position in the Seattle area. Our flights had timed up. My arriving flight from Alaska landed an hour-and-a-half before his took off to San Francisco. I was supposed to simply leave my gate and meet him there. Instead of getting off the N-gate train to the C-gate (which is the closest gate to the food court), for some reason I simply got off at baggage claim (I still, to this day, don't know what the heck I was thinking).

When I passed security, I quickly realized what I had done. My heart stopped and that warm blanket of fear, frustration, panic, and embarrassment crept across my body. I couldn't get back into the terminal. I asked the security guard if she'd allow me back into the train loading dock. She shook her head and said, "Not a chance." I frantically grabbed my cell phone and first texted, then called the hiring manager to see if he could come back into the check-in area.

Obviously annoyed, he answered back on the other line, with a cold stern voice, "Sorry, but I can't come back through. Maybe this isn't the right fit. Good luck, Collin."

Dumped before even meeting my date.

Upset and feeling rejected, I left the airport parking lot in a rage, gripping the steering wheel tightly. With each mile passed on the highway, a new negative thought popped into my head: *Maybe the recruiters are right. . . . Maybe I've been in my role for too long. . . . Do I have what it takes to change industries? . . . Will I ever find a role at work that I love? . . . How long will I live like this?* I went down the list: I felt unfulfilled and operating as just a shell of my best self.

I had put a great deal of importance on that interview because I was in a rut, a mental and emotional dark hole.

Have you ever taken a moment to reflect if you are maxing out your potential on a scale from zero to 100? I have. At that time I was completely aware that I was under performing. I remember thinking to myself that I was only operating around 30% of what I was capable of.

Rate yourself right now from 0-100%. Where are you on the Potential Scale? Are you maximizing your full potential mentally, physically, and spiritually?

Let me explain why I labeled my effectiveness at 30%. I was six-plus years into a career as a medical sales professional. Through my professional climb, I had worked my way up to the elevated role of an oncology account manager. I had a high base salary, autonomy, and my position was very specialized serving a niche in the cancer community.

Like many things in life, *timing* and *placement* are everything. Unfortunately, those two forces were working against me. Let's start with timing. The company I was working for (which I loved for my first four or five years) had recently changed their compensation plan to be heavily weighted on manager appraisals, surveys, and written and verbal tests over the phone. I felt lost and discouraged in this new structure. Instead of being paid for growing revenue and generating product orders, they were paying us on regional customer feedback and our ability to answer unrealistic questions from some phone operator I've never met.

How do you think that affected morale—especially mine? Not well, that's for sure.

Now with placement. I quickly learned that access to speak to oncologists and their nurses was quite challenging. In my previous role as a respiratory specialist, I was used to seeing four to eight accounts a day. In my oncology role, I was lucky to have one real face-to-face visit per week.

Recognizing that my role, and the compensation structure for that matter, wasn't the right fit for me, I dreamed of leaving that role and getting into a new position. I had some earlier opportunities to make the jump, but my self-sabotaging mindset of playing it safe, imposter syndrome, and staying comfortable with what I knew kept me from taking that leap.

I hit my limit, though. I needed to get out of my internal and external cage. I was dealing with several metaphorical chains. The heaviest and most taxing was my anxiety based on perfectionism. I cared so much about my image. I gave myself no margin for error and received my validation from how I interpreted what people thought of me. A byproduct of this perfectionism was a mild stutter that I hid for years.

What you avoid, you attract, after all. What you don't use, you lose.

I saw my fluency and confidence hit all-time lows due to a lack of customer interactions.

It's like a baseball hitter rarely getting batting practice to prepare for games. My lack of live reps reviewing my product created anxiety when it came time to present to physicians, nurses, and pharmacists. I lacked the repetitions with customers that I was used to.

Though the challenge of learning new complex disease states, mastering oncology terminology, and adjusting to a slower selling cycle was very challenging, it really came down to one thing: The phone assessments killed me. These mandated verbal tests were extremely stressful. Before my first verbal test in this new system, I had to take a Xanax just to help calm myself down. It didn't work. Imagine if your mortgage payment came down to how well you could say scientific words and correctly answer made-up unrealistic scenarios over the phone. Oh, add performance anxiety and a stuttering problem to the mix. I was a stumbling, mumbling, sputtering mess. I had what baseball players call "a case of the yips." The yips are a mental block that hinders your ability to execute a simple task that you used to do in the past (for example, not being able to throw the ball back to the pitcher). In my case, my yips were not being able to answer questions over the phone without stuttering.

This combination of a lack of job fulfillment and verbal testing amplified my anxiety, which caused a cascade of negative effects: high blood pressure that required medication, horrible nights sleeping, and a lack of self worth. During this stressful season, I reached out to a counselor. I was too nervous to call her on the phone, so I sent her an email. The subject line read: "Confidence Coach."

She was confused with what I meant, but I scheduled an appointment anyway. During our third session I realized that analyzing my past was not helping my current state or confidence (in hindsight, I should have stuck with it, and for the record, I'm a big advocate for counseling and therapy).

Feeling that I was running out of options, the interview at the airport seemed like a way out. Missing it was the straw that broke the camel's back. Yet in this case, it was my spirit that was broken.

After Kendra and I returned from our walk outside on the trail where I had a physical and emotional nervous breakdown, we came back inside and I sat at my desk in our office. I opened my laptop and was about to fire up Medreps.com to see if I could apply for another medical sales opening in Seattle. While I was waiting to connect to the internet, I started to unpack my backpack from my trip. The first thing I pulled out was a book that I hadn't touched in three months. My manager had gifted everyone on the team the book *Positive Intelligence*, by Shirzad Chamine. It literally just sat in my backpack untouched.

I'll read it on one of my work trips to Anchorage, I told myself when I first received this gift.

That never happened.

During that time in my life, I was more interested in movies, Netflix, and watching sports than investing in my personal development.

Man, this Internet is frickin' slow, I thought to myself while waiting for my wireless connection.

While I sat there in my office waiting for the four Internet bars on my laptop screen to light up, I opened up *Positive Intelligence* and began to read the first page.

Might as well pass the time, I figured.

One minute turned into 10 minutes. 10 minutes turned into an hour. I was hooked. That moment brought me to this truth,

When the student is ready, the teacher appears.

I was no doubt the student and desperate to learn.

Kendra interrupted my focus by calling me upstairs for dinner *(side note: I have the best wife on the planet. I'm so grateful for her patience and support)*.

After dinner and putting the kids to bed, I jumped back in my office and into the content that I felt was written for me. Have you ever read a book, quote, or met someone that helped make better sense of life? This book did that for me. The author, Shirzad Charmine, believes that we all have this negative inner-voice that he calls our "judge." This judge and critic is served by mental saboteurs, or what Dr. Brené Brown calls our inner "gremlins." Each individual has particular saboteurs specific to them. My internal gremlins were extra loud for most of my life, including my time as a two-sport, division-I student-athlete.

I finally realized that I'm not my brain and that our mind is actually designed to survive, not thrive. It was my job to take control of my life through self-awareness, grace, discipline, and by practicing productive self-talk. I learned that I was in control. I had the ability to influence my environment with my thoughts, not the other way around.

It all comes down to this question: Who is leading who? Similar to a person walking a dog. Is the owner walking the dog or is the dog walking the owner? I often let my brain lead me instead of me lead my brain.

The mental skills I learned in *Positive Intelligence* shifted my focus and gave me direction. I received the guidance needed to begin the personal work on myself that I had been delaying and avoiding. I later learned this process is what one of the founders of Cognitive Behavioral Therapy (CBT), Dr. David D. Burns, calls "bibliotherapy." Meaning, through powerful self-help books written by clinical and applied psychology experts, you can learn to improve your thoughts, moods, and habits through a series of self-awareness, cognitive, and behavior modifications (check out Burns' book *Feel Good*... it's phenomenal). I had never really read personal development books tied to mindset like that before. To say it was impactful would be an understatement.

It took me about two weeks to finish the book, and a funny thing happened the following day I received a phone call from a medical device recruiter. I remember exactly where I was. I was standing in the Issaquah Swedish hospital lobby right next to their long and skinny fireplace. The recruiter's name was Doug, and he had a rich, smooth voice that reminded me of Ron Burgundy from the film *Anchorman*.

Thank God for LinkedIn, I thought to myself as I sat down on a nearby black leather couch in the lobby, while Doug walked me through the role on the phone. As he talked, I was taking notes frantically trying to capture every detail. The opening was in the urology division of Bard Medical, and I imagined my newfound recruiter friend on the other end of the phone in a turtleneck and thick mustache as he filled me in on the company, products, and marketplace.

After developing a game plan from Doug and shifting my mindset, I had a newfound confidence stepping into the phone and live interviews. The aim was to just be authentically myself and quiet my inner-citric with positive and affirming language. After my final interview in Covington, Georgia, I remember receiving the phone call that changed my life and set me on a new trajectory. It was from the hiring manager informing me that I got the job (I love you, Mike Mersinger). Standing by my hotel bed and still in my best dark suit and navy tie, I started pumping my fist and smiling from ear to ear.

I was so fired up. I felt like I had just left a jail sentence—emotionally from the role I was in, and mentally from living in a constant state of self-doubt and fear. I was so ready to embark on a new journey into a world that I had forgotten—freedom, autonomy, and the exciting new challenge of endless possibilities. I felt like a chained carnivore that was finally let out of its cage, ready to attack whatever it is that it wanted. What I wanted was to feel fulfilled again and to finally take the steps necessary to reach my full potential.

That experience set the stage for my obsession with mental conditioning and performance psychology. To make a long story short, since that fateful tantrum by the pond, I have worked tirelessly to transform myself. Through this process I have tried to consume as many books, podcasts, research studies, TED talks, and YouTube videos on the power of the mind that I can (I have an extensive list you'll see later in this book). In my car, doing chores, going on walks, and reading at home—I developed a deep passion for learning, applying, and teaching mental skills. I've taken a variety of courses and earned multiple mental performance certifications to strengthen my knowledge to really focus on the applied side of mental conditioning—not just theory—and making myself the test subject.

The tools I learned in this process have flat out worked and upgraded my life personally and professionally.

With a new company and mental toolkit, I set sales records and earned top five and number one national finishes. I annually won President Club Awards, including trips to Greece and Tahiti. With this success I was promoted to National Sales Trainer, teaching sales psychology, success habits, and mental performance skills to new hires and veteran reps across the country. I remember wondering, *Why are these mental skills not actively taught in schools, sports and with working adults?* Most of the focus on mental fitness is on rehab, but not prehab.

I was on a mission to change that.

With these transformational learnings, I started blogging on the power of mindset. This grew into writing multiple books and then designing performance journals, online courses, individual and group coaching programs, and curriculum for businesses, athletic teams, and school districts. I was juggling two full-time jobs for several years—mental performance coaching and medical sales. Not being able to keep up both roles, I left corporate America and started my own company, Master Your Mindset. I discovered that was my true calling.

Over the last several years running my company, I've been blessed to train the most successful companies in the world including Zillow, Amazon, Nike, Microsoft, Salesforce, Paychex, and lululemon (I'm also a proud lululemon ambassador... we have the best people and gear in the business!). In addition, I've been trusted to provide mindset training to college, club, high school sports teams, and school districts all over the country. Most importantly though, I've become a better husband and father to our now five children. That is my proudest accomplishment.

Though I have grown so much, I'm probably more proud of my resume of failures during this transformation process. I've faced my fears and challenged many of my old limiting beliefs. It was at times excruciating, but definitely worth it.

Along this journey, I have realized that the biggest competition I will ever face is myself. It's me versus me. It's you versus you. Our own brain and conditioning often stand in the way of our dreams. I want to help you override your natural negative internal wiring, just like I try to do each day.

In this book, my intent is to help you get out of your own way, gain clarity on what you want, and build a system to get there. The goal is to find inner-peace, calmness, confidence, and to maximize the most powerful tool you have: **your mind.**

To help you train a quiet mind, I've broken down the fundamentals of thinking and provide a 10 chapter blueprint to condition your mindset to be more fit, just like your body. It all comes down to thoughtful design and repetitions, which I'll outline in the next chapter.

I'll end this intro with one of my favorite quotes from author and philosopher Joseph Campbell. He once said,

"The cave you fear to enter holds the treasure that you seek."

That's so profound and true. I'm living proof.

If I can do it, you can do it. Let's go!

MENTAL WARM-UP
MINDSET FUNDAMENTALS

While conducting workshops, seminars, and coaching sessions, one of the first questions I like to ask as a mental warmup is this: What is your definition of mindset?

Take a moment to give that question some thought. How would you define the word "mindset?" Using the space below (and without peeking ahead), break that concept down in your own words:

Here's my definition of mindset: **A <u>conditioned</u> set of <u>beliefs</u> that drive <u>behavior</u>.**

It's through your conditioning (whether you are aware of it or not) that influences your inner and outer beliefs. These beliefs directly influence your habits, actions, and performance in life.

MINDSET:

A CONDITIONED SET OF BELIEFS THAT DRIVE BEHAVIOR

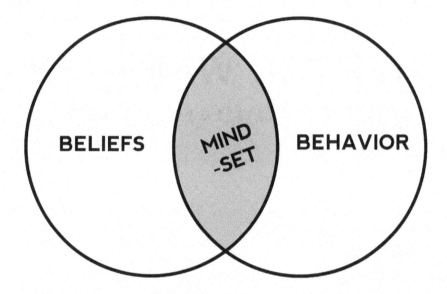

Here is another way to explain it.

Do you have a junk drawer in your house? Think of that spot... maybe in your kitchen, your bathroom, or your garage. It's that one location that's filled with all your random items that have slowly piled up and are not organized whatsoever.

Can you think of a time when you needed to use an essential object to complete a task—like some tape, scissors, or a pen? When you went to that junk drawer and rummaged around trying to find that tool, you eventually walked away feeling frustrated, because it was nowhere to be found. We've all been there, right?

Well, your brain is a lot like that junk drawer. You have been storing thoughts, emotions, experiences, and fears your entire life. If you are like most people, you just keep adding items in that mental junk drawer with no structure, system, or intent to remove the crap that is useless and does not serve you.

These items of clutter in your mind take the form of images, beliefs, and feelings you've experienced since childhood.

Let's break down the basic structure of your brain that stores these emotions (I'll do my best to simplify this).

- Found in the frontal lobe, the prefrontal cortex plays a large role in personality development, motivation, and executive functions including focus, managing emotions, planning, and coordinating complex behaviors.
- The limbic system is one of the first parts of the brain to develop because its purpose is centered around behavioral and emotional responses tied to survival—as in hunger and fight or flight responses
- The amygdala is the fear center, which is found in the middle of the brain. It signals the prefrontal cortex when there is danger, a threat, or stressful environment
- The hippocampus is part of the limbic system and is in charge of learning, memory, and emotional regulation
- The spinal cord and nervous system—central and peripheral—coordinate homeostasis, memory, and sensory information by transmitting signals to and from different parts of its body that influence motor reflexes
- The hypothalamus has widespread effects on behavior from the release of hormones, which sends signals to either stimulate or to relax different functions of the body
- The cerebrum is the large outer part of the brain and controls thinking, learning, speech, emotions, while controlling vision, hearing and other senses
- The cerebellum is in charge of coordination and voluntary movements such as posture, balance, and muscular activity

Unfortunately, these compartments of the brain are prone to hold onto negative emotions and store them. This "conditioning" often shapes our perspective, expectations, self-image, and response to perceived threats.

If I were to ask, "How do you see the world? Or, how do you see yourself?" What would you say? Your internal picture and perspective are often shaped less by positive experiences and more from what I call: **Trauma, Drama, Daddy and Mama.**

- Trauma – painful experiences of distress causing severe mental and emotional harm
- Drama – stressful relationships or environments
- Daddy & Mama – conditioning from your parents and upbringing

This conditioning is shaped by three factors: what we see, what we hear, and what we experience. Our negative internal perception is due to the brain's hyper-focus of survival and acceptance. That's why I created this book, as sort of a brain healing blueprint.

Here's an example: Imagine going to IKEA and buying a new piece of furniture. You take it home all excited, you have the spot ready to go in your house, but when you open the box, it doesn't have the directions, manual, or tools to piece the items together. That's how most of us are living our life. We have the pieces, but not the right guide. I want to help you recondition your mind to let go, heal, start fresh, and rebuild your brain with the right user's manual and tools.

Back to the junk drawer analogy, do this exercise with me. Pretend you are removing your brain from your head just like you would remove your junk drawer from the counter. Now DUMP THE CONTENTS OUT! It's time to put your brain back in your head like you would an empty drawer with a clean slate. This is where things get exciting. Let's turn this junk drawer (aka your brain) into a mental and emotional toolkit that helps you solve problems, not create them.

As your mindset coach, I'm going to help you organize your mind with specific mental skills and tools that you will train, so you can go to these tools when you need them. My hope is that there will be no confusion as to where to look within yourself and find these mental skills:

- Confidence
- Authenticity
- Resilience
- Consistency
- Poise
- Focus
- Optimism
- Compassion

When you know what you need and where to find it, there is very little thinking involved. Through this process of awareness, practice, and clarity, you will think better and become more. Let's re-organize your brain and develop a quiet mind.

Optimal Thinking

With the aim of building inner-peace, follow this sequence: Bad thoughts are bad, good thoughts are good, but no thought is best.

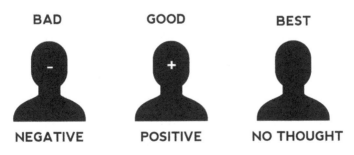

We cannot reach our full potential through constant negative thinking. Training neutral to productive thoughts are a gateway to a quiet mind.

In best-selling author Ryan Holiday's book, *Stillness is the Key*, he writes, "There is a violent Civil War raging within each and every person."

Who is winning the fight within you?
How loud and cluttered is your internal world?

The truth is, no one can completely shut off negative thoughts from popping up. That's not the goal. The goal is to minimize the frequency, intensity, and have a plan to respond. This is what Harvard psychologist, TED speaker, and best selling author, Susan David, explores in her book *Emotional Agility*. Dr. David believes, "Emotions are data, they are not directives." She also adds, "Discomfort is the price of admission to a meaningful life."

Here's one more philosophical concept to consider from Dr. David, she asks, "Who is in charge, the thinker or the thought?"

It's time to finally take ownership of your mind and not let your limiting beliefs and past negative conditioning hold you back. We all have access to the power of free will. Though it can feel challenging and scary, you are in control of you.

In order to improve this psychological strength, you must do what Mental Skills Coordinator with the Philadelphia Phillies, Hannah Huesman, likes to say: get your "mental sweat" on. You are in the right place to do just that (side note: Hannah is a great follow on Instagram and LinkedIn for a ton of mindset tips).

The Why

I developed this workbook for several reasons. The first is because I know what it feels like to be in a mental rut. For many years I was my own worst enemy because of my negative internal voice. As a former Division I two-sport athlete and sales professional, my biggest competition wasn't an opponent, but my own negative self-talk. I'd often get in my own way by replaying past mistakes, thinking worst-case scenarios (example: don't drop it, don't strikeout, don't screw up, don't stutter, everyone's judging me, etc.), and placing my energy on things outside of my control. I would get consumed by my perception of other people's opinions, chasing the lie of perfection, and worrying about future outcomes. I often had what is called "imposter syndrome," in which I felt I did not belong or was unworthy of greatness.

I remember during a TV timeout while playing college football as a wide receiver in the Pac-12 Conference at Washington State University (Go Cougs!), I found myself sizing up my opponent, in this case, the strong safety across from me. It was a cold November night in Pullman, Washington. With light snow falling on the green turf of Martin Stadium, these were my thoughts: *His arms look as big as my thighs. How am I supposed to block him, let alone get open? What am I doing out here?*

Not the most productive thought process, huh?

What about you? Do you have unproductive thoughts and distracting internal noise, like the ones listed below?
- Comparing
- Worrying what others think
- Perfectionism
- Replaying mistakes
- Fearing failure

- Trying to please everyone and be liked

These internal roadblocks are your real opponent.

These types of limiting beliefs definitely held me back. I could execute in practice, but often lacked consistency and could not maintain that high level of performance in games or in specific sales situations. This perfectionism and fear of failure carried over into a phobia of public speaking that plagued me for years.

As I mentioned in the introduction, before I founded my company, Master Your Mindset, and became a full-time peak performance consultant, I spent over a decade in medical sales as a rep and sales trainer. During the first half of my sales career, my confidence was like a roller coaster. I'd have times where I could execute at a high level and other times where my limiting beliefs and fears got the best of me—specifically around speaking with confidence. My fluency was sometimes erratic since grade school. I went through many different rounds of speech therapy in my youth and as a young adult to help me overcome a lisp and slight stammer.

I remember one time when my nerves completely sabotaged my performance. It was during an online Webex regional meeting. I was sitting in my black Ford Escape SUV company car in a Target parking lot, while using my laptop and mobile hotspot to connect. When it was my turn to speak to the attendees, I experienced a sudden panic attack—my heart was pounding uncontrollably, I felt a tingling warmth all over my body, and my vocal cords squeezed shut. I could barely breathe. In this moment of panic, I slammed my computer shut. I didn't even utter one word. I sent a text to my manager: "So sorry . . . my mobile hotspot isn't working."

That was an example of a common headspace for me at work—feeling extremely insecure, fearing failure, and losing control of my internal state. I had too many moments like this to count.

Can you think of a similar experience that happened to you, when fear or self-doubt got the best of you?

Due to my stuttering trauma and fears, there were times in my life when I struggled answering the phone, ordering food through a drive-through, and even saying my name. I have a deep sense of compassion and empathy for those who are managing self-doubt, self-worth, and anxiety because I have lived it.

The other inspiration for this workbook came from a request I received from a Minor League manager for a Major League Baseball organization. He was in Arizona for spring training with his team and was seeking counsel on any tips to help a player and coach with the yips. The yips is a term used to classify a mental block that is impeding one's ability to perform a simple physical task. In this case, one of his players and coaches were struggling throwing the baseball in specific situations. I told him there are no simple quick fixes, but I would put together a plan that, if executed consistently (just like a workout or diet plan), the individuals seeking help would position themselves in a positive way to see improvements. I have expanded that mental program to what you see in front of you now.

Negative Bias

I've spent years digging deep into the field of mental performance because of a) having a heart to serve performers of all types (like the example above) and b) dealing with my own internal struggles. A key finding I've learned is that our brain is often working against us.

A 2005 study from the National Science Foundation found that 80% of human thoughts are negative and 95% of thoughts are recurring. Did you catch that? In the untrained mind, four out of five thoughts are negative (Wow—that's nuts!). In other words, we have an ancient brain in modern times that is designed to survive, not thrive. Thankfully, we are no longer being hunted by predators in the wild.

Our fears of survival and physical safety have shifted to what high performance psychologist Michael Gervais calls "FOPO" (Fear of Other People's Opinions). Our fear of failure and what other people think of our performance robs us of joy, creativity, being present in the moment, and thus falling short of our full potential. The goal is to have a different type of FOPO, which is Freedom of Other People's Opinions. This type of internal peace takes extreme self-compassion and clarity.

"FOPO"

FEAR OF OTHER PEOPLE'S OPINIONS

"FOPO IS THE #1 KILLER OF PERFORMANCE TODAY"
— DR. MICHAEL GERVAIS — PERFORMANCE PSYCHOLOGIST

Another way I often explain how our thoughts can help or hurt us is an example from an old parable—one I try to fit into all my books and presentations as a quick and powerful mindset reminder. As the story goes, there are two wolves fighting inside our brain, a Good Wolf and a Bad Wolf. The Bad Wolf is negative and says things like, "You're not good enough . . . everyone's watching . . . you can't do it . . . you will fail . . . you better succeed or else . . . you don't belong here."

Conversely, the Good Wolf is optimistic and says things like, "You are worthy . . . you got this . . . I believe in you . . . you can improve . . . go for it!"

WHICH WOLF WINS?

THE GOOD ONE

THE BAD WOLF

STRENGTHS	WEAKNESSES
WHAT I HAVE	WHAT I DON'T HAVE
I SEE SUCCESS	I SEE FAILURE
OPTIMISM	PESSIMISM
"I'VE GOT THIS!"	"DON'T SCREW UP!"

IF YOU THINK YOU ARE OR YOU AREN'T
— YOU'RE RIGHT!

So which wolf wins this fight? The answer is: The one that you feed. What internal wolf have you been feeding? Your brain believes what it is told most.

Here's another question to ponder for a second: What does the word "wolf" spell backwards?

The answer is: *FLOW.*

"Flow" is a term coined by one of the founding fathers of positive psychology, Dr. Mihaly Csikszentmihalyi. Flow means "being in the zone." Flow is the most optimal state we can be in as humans. In this peaceful quiet state, we are completely present, not judging, there is no sense of time, and the activity is the reward, not the outcome. Focus, productive thinking, feeling a sense of challenge, and having a clear goal are gateways to flow. But, you cannot and will not enter a flow state by being pessimistic and negative.

BAD IS STRONGER THAN GOOD

NEGATIVITY IS 4-7X STRONGER THAN POSITIVITY
—DR. CHRISTINE PORATH

Dr. Christine Porath, researcher and business professor at Georgetown University, notes the "negative of negative," and that "bad is stronger than good." Her research shows that speaking negatively has four to seven times more power over being positive. When you break that down, it takes roughly four to seven positive thoughts or words to counter just one internal or external soundbite of negativity.

According to Harvard Business Review, a similar positive to negative ratio is also found in groups. When looking at high performing teams, researchers found that the ratio of positive comments to negative comments was 5.6 to 1. For moderately performing teams it was 1.9 to 1. And the low performing team's positive to negative ratio was 0.36 to 1.

See a correlation? What is the positive to negative ratio within your team?

What about the positive to negative ratio in your own mind?

Why is this even important? According to Chad Bohling, Director of Mental Conditioning with the New York Yankees and Dallas Cowboys, "The right attitude is a competitive advantage."

Inner-Voice

The human brain is amazing. We generate around 70,000 thoughts per day. Our subconscious mind never shuts off. Between 95-97% of human behavior is controlled by these subconscious thoughts and beliefs. Being more aware of this internal voice and negative patterns are extremely powerful. According to renowned mental conditioning consultant, Trevor Moawad—whose client list includes the University of Georgia Football, New York Mets, Goldman Sachs, and Johnson & Johnson, among others—"What you say to yourself is 10 times more powerful than what anyone can say to you."

Moawad is the founder and co-chairman of the corporate mindset training group, Limitless Minds. I have the privilege of collaborating with their innovative team as a mental conditioning consultant and have learned a ton working within this organization (much love to Harry, DJ, Trevor, Matt, Russell, Amanda, David, Catherine, Ana, and the rest of the squad!).

One of my favorite tools Moawad teaches is the importance of developing an internal "advertising campaign" for yourself. Just like a business would market their product to consumers with slogans and taglines, you should practice influencing yourself on your own value proposition as well.

Reflect on this: Do you talk yourself into peak performance or do you talk yourself out of being your best due to fear and negativity?

This ad campaign tactic of "thought replacement"—intentionally blocking and substituting unproductive thoughts with productive ones—will help offset the brain's bias for being negative and will influence a more focused performance.

Take a look at the thought replacement practice of one of Moawad's most well-known clients and partner at Limitless Minds, Pro Bowl and Super Bowl-winning quarterback Russell Wilson. When Wilson is mic'd up for games, his self-talk sounds like this on repeat:

"I am here.
I'm built for this.
Stay Neutral.
Believe!
Why not us?"

In 2019, Wilson became the highest paid player in NFL history that year. He sees the value in conditioning his mindset, as it helps raise his performance—especially when the game is on the line. Since 2012, no NFL quarterback has had more fourth quarter or overtime comebacks than Wilson. He knows that executing under pressure has as much to do with mental skills as physical skills. Wilson likes to say, "If we train the body, shouldn't we train the mind?"

Wilson and many other experts believe in the power of owning your words and thoughts. The human performance group, The Mindstrong Project, founded by my friend, Harvey Martin, says that our internal voice sets off a chain reaction that influences our performance. See the sequence below.

THOUGHTS influence EMOTIONS influence BIOCHEMISTRY influence ACTIONS influence PERFORMANCE.

THOUGHT CASCADE

THOUGHTS
↓
EMOTIONS
↓
BIOCHEMISTRY
↓
ACTIONS
↓
PERFORMANCE

"WE BECOME WHAT WE THINK
ABOUT MOST OF THE TIME"
— EARL NIGHTINDALE

Lou Tice, one of my heroes and founders of one of the first high performance mindset consulting companies, The Pacific Institute (based in Seattle), echoes these truths. He used to say, "The brain thinks in three dimensions... in words, pictures, and feelings."

Envisioning worst-case scenarios and replaying past mistakes through words and mental pictures, alter our internal activation levels (elevated heart rate, shallow breathing, tight muscles, etc.), which impedes our ability to be confident and present in the moment. The brain produces the same fear response to social threats and it does physical safety threats. This negative mental and physical state hinders us from executing something we have either performed before or can potentially perform without pressure. I call this overthinking "micro-managing." Similar to the phrase "paralysis by analysis," we drain precious mental and physical energy, and fall short of our potential. I used to be an expert at that—judging and critiquing my every step. I would judge my performance from the outside-in (what I thought people would see) versus inside-out (what I see and experience).

Does that sound familiar?

According to Steven Kotler, a flow expert and best-selling author of *The Rise of Superman* and *The Art of Impossible*, the brain makes up only 2% of our body mass, but burns around 25% of our energy. When we are overly stressed, angry, and confused, we burn more fuel and fatigue sets in.

If you are suffering from FOPO, negative self-talk, replaying mistakes, anticipating failure, or an elevated biochemistry that is hindering your performance, please know you are not alone. Everyone deals with bouts here and there, whether in one's career or just throughout life. Because you are human, no one is immune to worry or doubt. Nerves are actually quite normal. This spike of internal activation can actually help you perform better—with the right training, of course.

Unfortunately, there are no quick fixes. Just like strengthening your muscles or learning a new skill, it takes time and daily repetitions. To get stronger physically, you wouldn't simply go to the gym once and expect to become more fit. Mental training is the same way. You must commit to improve your inner-voice, give yourself compassion (like you would a teammate, coworker, family member, or friend), and change your daily habits to foster the right mindset, so you can take control of your internal state and get out of your own way.

Anything worthwhile in life does not come easy. I've never met a strong person who has had an easy past. Quick fixes and hacks don't create lasting change. If that's what you want from this book, you won't find it. A speaker or author doesn't magically change people. You have to do the work to change yourself.

WHICH DOOR?

Have faith. Because of the phenomenon of neuroplasticity, you can literally change your brain through new thought patterns and habits. To execute this, you have to do what the Star Wars character Yoda says: "You must unlearn what you have learned."

The basic premise of this book that we are authoring together, is this: You act, train, work, and behave not in accordance with the truth, but your perception of the truth. You will learn that if you can change the way you think and see yourself, you will change the way you act and perform.

To help you own your truth, improve your self-talk, self-image, and thought-mosphere (aka your thought-life), I've developed a confidence-boosting system to help you lower unproductive stress, shift perspective, feel more in control, and be in the present moment—which is the holy grail of peak performance. I've used this system to help correct my former stuttering problem (which I still work on daily), as well as a phobia of public speaking. By learning and implementing the skills I'm about to teach you, I now coach audiences in the thousands to make similar strides.

This system includes the following ten plays (think of this as an offensive system), broken into chapters, to help you feed the Good Wolf and get out of your own way. Stop playing defense with your mental game. Start playing offense and develop a quiet mind.

Play I: Self-Awareness
Clarity is power

Play II: Be Open
You don't need to be sick to get better / Asking for help is a sign of strength

Play III: Perspective
Your job, sport, or activity is a "get to" not a "have to"... you are not defined by it

Play IV: Priming
Before you begin your day, prime your mind, just like your body

Play V: Power of Process
Develop a plan and specific routines that create confidence, consistency, and a sense of calm

Play VI: Optimal Performance State
Set yourself up for success by getting into a peak state before and during times of performance

Play VII: Frame Your Focus
Learn how to focus on what you can control

Play VIII: Reset
Have a plan for when adversity strikes

Play IX: Recovery & Reflection
True learning and growth happen upon reflection and rest, not during the activity

Play X: Become Limitless
One of the best investments you can make is upgrading your knowledge and beliefs daily through self-improvement habits

In this current era of data, distractions, noise, and information overload... quieting your mind is the new currency of success.

By taking the time to gain clarity, self-awareness, and front load your thinking through learning these 10 mental skills, you will set yourself up to do less thinking when it's time to perform. Practice these plays until the plays run themselves.

According to one of the godfather's of mental conditioning and author of *Coaching the Mental Game*, Harvey Dorfman, he says transformation comes down to three simple steps called **A.S.A. (Awareness. Strategy. Action.).** This book follows a similar structure:

1. **Awareness** – with the learnings, prompts, and reflective questioning, gain the knowledge to better understand your thoughts, beliefs, and behaviors.

2. **Systems** – With a newfound sense of self-awareness, develop a process and routines that you will execute consistently.

3. **Application** – Get your reps in and implement your new learnings and systems daily. By implementing your plan, you will see transformation and sustained peak performance.

It's time to take ACTION! Open your calendar right now and schedule your *Quiet Mind* mental workouts (as in, reading this book, reflecting, taking notes, developing your plan, and implementing these strategies). Just like you would schedule your hike, weightlifting, spin class, CrossFit, Orange Theory, or yoga session—what days and times will you condition your mind? Get in a small group and do this training with a partner. Who will you include in your mental fitness journey?

A.S.A.
3 STEPS TO TRANSFORMATION

AWARENESS   SYSTEMS   APPLICATION

Let's get after it and build your *Quiet Mind* plan!

PLAY I
SELF-AWARENESS

Tennis legend Billie Jean King once said, "I think self-awareness is probably the most important thing towards being a champion."

But why is self-awareness so important? Here's why:

Awareness precedes behavior change.

You have the power to be your best coach. With this in mind, one of my favorite exercises to help my athlete and business clients master their mindset is to ask a series of questions dealing with self-awareness.

I have them reflect on past performances and describe times when they were experiencing the following:
- Feeling extreme joy;
- Performing at their highest level; and
- Having clarity and conviction.

I can vividly remember working through this exercise with a Division I basketball player who was in a funk. After a group mindset session I led in the team meeting room, Harper, a freshman starter, came up to me with her head down expressing that she was lacking confidence and overthinking everything. She shared that she was performing way under her ability and didn't know what to do.

I told her that it was completely normal to feel doubt and that I wanted to ask her a few questions to help her gain clarity. With a hopeful look in her eye, Harper said, "I'm willing to do anything."

One of the questions I asked her was to describe what it felt like when she played basketball on the street with her sister and neighborhood friends as a child and early teen. Harper explained how she didn't worry about her mistakes, was ruthlessly competitive, and would have a blast in that setting.

I asked, "What's holding you back from being in that frame of mind now?"

She expressed letting the pressure of a new environment, elevated expectations, and worrying about what others think (as in coaches, family, friends, and media) cloud her confidence. She committed to work on getting back to that mindset from her youth. Together, we came up with the phrase "just play." Instead of thinking about the pressure, her aim was to "just play." With this self-awareness work, Harper completely adjusted her mindset. We worked on several keys to shift her focus:

- The game of basketball is a get-to, not a have-to.
- Instead of worrying about the future, her goal was to be completely present.
- She vowed to compete to be her best, rather than compare herself to others.
- Instead of letting fear get the best of her, she began to retrain her brain to have fun again.

WHAT DO YOU FOCUS ON?

PLAY MINDSET	PRESSURE MINDSET
"I GET TO"	"I HAVE TO"
IMPROVE MYSELF	PROVE MYSELF
COMPETE VS MYSELF	COMPARE VS OTHERS
FOCUS ON FUN	FOCUS ON FEAR
BE PRESENT	PAST/FUTURE

Performance psychologist and author of, *Success: How We Can Reach Our Goals,* Heidi Grant, calls this perspective shift an "improve mindset" versus a "prove mindset." The aim is to focus on **improving** yourself each practice or competition instead of **proving** yourself. The latter is utterly exhausting and a performance killer.

Harper worked all week to apply these quiet mind truths in practice. It was so cool seeing her just a week later in a post-game press conference after having a career-high in points and rebounds sharing her new mindset epiphany. Sitting down at the press table with a Gatorade bottle and microphone in front of her, a reporter asked her to explain her exceptional performance. Harper said, "I was in my head earlier this season, and working with my mental coach, Collin, I got back to *just playing.*"

I was so proud and happy for her. That's self-awareness at its finest! Now it is your turn to unlock your own internal awareness, wisdom, and un-limited power.

Know Thyself

Just like a strength coach or personal trainer would do a series of baseline assessments to measure your strength, explosion, or speed early in your training process... as your mental performance coach, I'd like to guide you through a baseline assessment to create a starting point to work from.

Take a moment to reflect on your mental state in the past month, quarter, or year.

Baseline Question #1: FOCUS

Where has your focus been? Think about these three time frames, and divide your focus into each category, making sure it adds up to 100%.

Past ___% Present ___% Future ___%

Are you replaying past mistakes or looking into the future playing the "what-if" game?

Before I started proactively working on my mindset, my breakdown looked like this: 50% past, 45% future, and only 5% in the present moment. I used to replay my mistakes on a loop and worry about failing in the future. I'm getting much better at staying present, which takes intentionality and daily work. Have you ever paused and assessed where your focus is most of the time?

Let's train our mind to stop reliving and pre-living each moment. It's been said that shame lives in the past and anxiety lives in the future. But, peak performance lives in the present moment. According to the author of the timeless book *Heads-Up Baseball: Playing the Game One Pitch at a Time*, by the late sports psychologist and mental skills pioneer Ken Ravizza, peak performers are in the present moment 80% of the time or more.

It's important to be where your feet are.

Baseline Question #2: SELF-TALK

How have your thoughts been? Divide your self-talk into two categories, making sure they add up to 100 percent.

Unproductive Self-Talk (feeding the Bad Wolf) ___%
Productive Self-Talk (feeding the Good Wolf) ___%

Put more simply, does your inner and outer language tend to be more productive and serve you *(I got this, I'm ready, let's do this)* or unproductive and hurt you *(What are they thinking of me, I hope I don't fail, I can't do this)?*

Let's add another layer to this model. Most people think that there are only two options with our thoughts—either positive or negative. This is not totally true. There actually is a middle ground, which we call at Limitless Minds, "neutral thinking." In a neutral mindset, you are not judging good or bad, but focusing on what's in your control and taking the next best step. Being neutral is grounded in the present moment. With this lens, we believe that: **Negative thoughts are bad. Positive thoughts are good. However, no thought or neutral thinking is most optimal** (especially during times of adversity).

We know that negativity is never the right option and being negative works every time—for the negative. On the flip side, sometimes when our circumstances are grim and really hard (like the pandemic and experi-

encing forced layoffs), having what some psychologists call "toxic positivity" can actually be harmful as well. Fake or unrealistic positivity can
create tension and build unrealistic expectations. While there are benefits
to being an optimist and engaging in positive thinking (which I am a big
fan of), toxic positivity can become harmful when it's insincere, forceful,
or delegitimizes real feelings of anxiety, fear, sadness, or hardship. In the
end, it all comes down to emotional intelligence (EQ) and empathy—for
self and others.

Imagine losing by 50 points in the fourth quarter and yelling, "Don't worry
team, we are going to win!" That language doesn't help anybody.

A neutral mindset is looking at each moment with a non-judgmental and
truthful lens that shifts one's focus to be more behavior-based versus
concocting false stories of the past and expecting a catastrophic or unrealistic future. A neutral approach would sound more like, "Let's keep
competing and give all we have until the end!"

Time to reflect:

Do you have a neutral mind or are you often either high or low?

Back to the original question... Divide your self-talk into two categories,
making sure they add up to 100 percent.

Unproductive Self-Talk (negative) ___%
Productive Self-Talk (neutral to positive) ___%

Be honest with yourself! This is just a baseline. If you need help in this
area, I got you. The aim of this book is to help you filter your thoughts
away from negativity and focus on being neutral to positive.

Baseline Question #3: TIME
There are three things we can train: our body, our technical skills, and our
mind. How often are you training your mindset?

Rate yourself below on a scale from 1 - 10 (1-low and 10-high) on how much time you have been investing in your mental fitness.

Low - 1 2 3 4 5 6 7 8 9 10 - High

When I ask this question, most people don't know how to assess this category other than noting meditation or mindfulness. While these are great tools, there is much more to improving your mental game than that. This can include journaling, doing visualization and imagery work. Setting and measuring goals or creating a vision board. Practicing gratitude. Using breathing techniques. Writing or verbalizing productive self-talk. Working with a peak performance coach, therapist, psychologist, or counselor. Reflecting and learning from your day. Taking intentional mindfulness breaks. Executing pre-performance and recovery routines. Creating and assessing your daily and weekly habit plan. Connecting with nature. Investing in your personal development beyond this book.

What are you currently doing to invest in your mental fitness?

I'll help you build this list throughout the book. Now it's time to do some self-scouting.

Baseline Question #4: YOUR BEST
Describe a time when you were performing at your absolute best (could be anytime in the past). Reflect and describe what your self-talk, focus, and routines were like.

Performance example(s):

Self-talk:

Focus (what were you thinking about and focusing on?):

Routines/Habits (what were your habits and routines leading up to and during the performance?):

What clues about yourself did you gather from that reflection exercise?

Baseline Question #5: YOUR WORST
Describe a time when you were underperforming and executing well below your potential (maybe that time is now). What were/are your self-talk, focus, and routines like?

Performance example(s):

Self-talk:

Focus (what were you often thinking about and focusing on?):

Negative patterns/routines/distractions (or, what productive habits were you NOT doing?):

What clues about yourself did you gather from that reflection exercise?

Baseline Question #6: WANT TO IMPROVE
Pick a specific area of your life and/or craft (job, career, or sport) in which you'd like to improve and execute at a higher level.

List here:

Why do you want to improve in this area:

Nice work! If you are a leader or a coach, use these questions to actively check in with your team members to help them elevate their mindset and self-awareness.

Now that we have a mental conditioning baseline, let's keep building.

Locus of Control

Do you have any friends, colleagues, or teammates that either:

1. Find a way to make an excuse, or
2. Find a way to make something positive happen?

Which option sounds more like you? This is what I know to be true: the top performers in the world take ownership of their actions. They understand that excellence is a choice and not by chance.

What's your perspective—do things happen to you or do things happen for you?

Does your attitude influence your environment or does your environment influence your attitude?

These questions reveal what psychologists call "locus of control."

Developed by psychologist Julian Rotter in the 1950s, locus of control is the degree to which people believe they have control over shaping the outcome or events in their lives, as opposed to external forces beyond their control. I'll explain.

LOCUS OF CONTROL

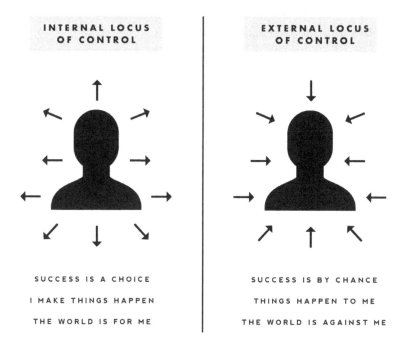

INTERNAL LOCUS OF CONTROL

SUCCESS IS A CHOICE

I MAKE THINGS HAPPEN

THE WORLD IS FOR ME

EXTERNAL LOCUS OF CONTROL

SUCCESS IS BY CHANCE

THINGS HAPPEN TO ME

THE WORLD IS AGAINST ME

Internal Locus of Control – Individuals with an internal locus of control believe, through their thoughts and actions, they have the power to control what happens to them in life, whether good or bad.

Like the old-school cartoon superhero He-Man used to say, "I have the POWER!"

External Locus of Control – Individuals with an external locus of control believe they cannot control their life, and their outcomes are decided by environmental and external factors, which they cannot influence. They believe success often comes down to luck and chance.

People with an external locus of control would make comments like this:
- "It's not my fault my sales are down, there's a back order."
- "We can't win here, our stadium and field are not as nice as other

programs."

- That person is successful because she was born intelligent and gifted. I'll never achieve the same level of success."

Whenever I hear statements like this it makes my skin crawl. Don't wait for luck, but make your own through hard work and belief!

Which describes you (circle one)?:

Internal locus of control   or   **External locus of control**

Reflect on which locus of control you chose. If you're unsure or lean toward external, it's time to reset those coordinates and take control of your actions. Below is a system that will help you do just that.

GPS

When GPS devices became commonplace in cars in the mid-2000s, they changed the way we drove and traveled. Just type the coordinates into a machine, and you magically hear a voice and see a path guiding you toward your destination.

I believe that living life without a clear vision and personal philosophy is just like driving without a GPS. Without a GPS, you are more likely to feel stuck, lost, and confused. What about when you are faced with detours and bumpy roads? Having a framework to guide your actions is critical to optimize your performance and build a quiet mind.

To help people on their path to mastery, I encourage them to create their own GPS, which stands for the following:

G – Guiding principles
P – Purpose statement
S – Slogan

Guiding Principles

Write down as many words as you can that are most important to you. How do you want to be remembered? What do you feel most strongly about? What traits do you value the most? What characteristics do your heroes and mentors have? Then limit your list to three to five words. Get clear on these core values. This is a crucial area of your life. And remember:

If you stand for nothing, you will fall for anything.

Example: NBA champion player and coach Steve Kerr's guiding principles are joy, compassion, mindfulness, and competition. A team I work with, Northern Arizona University Football—led by Coach Chris Ball, focus on #CHOP (they are the Lumberjacks) Character, Hardworking, Ownership, Present. Make your own list below:

-
-
-
-
-
-

Use these words to form how you will show up and act no matter the environment, situation, or who you are with. This process will help you shape your **character** and put these traits in action.

Purpose Statement

Not feeling motivated? Then it's time to find a new motive. I like to say, "The **goal** is the pull, but the **why** is the push." Why do you do what you do? Get clear on the reasons behind your actions. Your purpose statement can be a simple few words or a sentence. Don't overthink it. This exercise will help you find meaning in your effort. A simple way to uncover your purpose is to complete this sentence: My life's mission is _____. I want this goal **because** _____.

Your "because" becomes your motivation and purpose behind your actions. Or try these writing prompts:

- **That was for this**... as in, a struggle you went through that gives you the energy and drive to serve a larger purpose.
- **This is for that**... a reminder that your daily actions, effort, and hard work serve a person, group, or cause that is bigger than you—now or in the future.

Holocaust survivor, psychologist, and author of the moving book, *Man's Search for Meaning,* Dr. Viktor Frankl, said it best, "Those who have a 'why' to live can bear almost any 'how.'"

Example: Blake Mycoskie, the founder of TOMS Shoes, has a purpose statement (and business model) of "One for One." For every one pair of shoes his company sells, they give a pair of shoes to a child in need. Give it a shot. Write your purpose statement or "why" below.

Think of your **purpose** when you need a boost of motivation or inspiration to keep going when you are facing challenges.

Slogan

What's your mantra? What's your vision? What do you want to be known for? What do you want on your gravestone? What's a simple phrase that will help you take action?

Put together a two to five word sentence that can sum up your core beliefs. This slogan will provide clarity and help guide you, and those around you, along the road of success. Examples: Seattle Seahawks Head Coach Pete Carroll slogan is, "Always compete." Media mogul Oprah Winfrey's life motto is, "Live your best life." Write a few slogans down and pick the one that moves you the most.

Put this slogan on your email signature, social media platforms, and in your room or office. Let people know what you are all about! Use this system and clarity as a guide post for when you perform and experience new environments (socially and professionally).

Can you think of a moment when having your own internal GPS would have served you? The top leaders and performers in the world have extreme clarity and can say "yes" to all of these statements. I call this *living in alignment.*

- I know what I want.
- I know who I strive to be.

- I know what I stand for.

Can *you* say the same? This just might be the most important self-awareness exercise that helps you gain vision, meaning, and conviction.

Here's my GPS...

Guiding principles: Gratitude, Giving and Growing daily (I call this being a "G").
Purpose statement: Transform lives and normalize mental skills training.
Slogan: The body has limits, but the mind is limitless.

I end every single podcast, training video, virtual presentation, or Facebook and Instagram Live with my slogan. I also frequently use these taglines: "Thoughts become things," (#tbt) and "Let's Go!"

Clarity is power. The best focus on less, not more. Just like a GPS device, I want your brain to have this type of clear focus as well.

Now that you have a baseline, let's address some of the concerns you might have and build a daily plan not to run away from fear . . . but to attack it.

PLAY II
BE OPEN

I love this quote from mental performance pioneer and author of *Mind Gym*, Gary Mack, "The mind is like a parachute; it only works if it's open."

This is an easy concept in theory. However, being open and vulnerable to share your flaws, ask for help, and try something new is extremely hard. As a performer, you might get caught in the trap of saying, "That's how I/ we have always done it." Or, "I am who I am. I can't change." These statements are killers to innovation and creativity.

Saying and believing statements like this is having what Stanford professor and psychologist Carol Dweck calls a "fixed mindset." This concept is not new and is found in many other high performance resources, but it's worth a quick review. Fixed mindset individuals believe that talent and skill are fixed—that people are just born with it. They avoid challenges and feedback. They focus on image and outcomes only. When people have success, they feel threatened by it.

The opposite of a fixed mindset is what's called a "growth mindset." Individuals with this mindset believe that our brain, skills, and success can grow and are limitless. Growth mindset individuals are open to feedback and challenges. They value effort and improvement over outcomes, and celebrate when their peers do well. If you feel you lean more toward the fixed mindset, know that it's possible to develop yourself with the right perspective and habits.

Take a moment to reflect. *Have you been operating with a fixed or growth mindset?*

What is the biggest contributor to this roadblock of openness? I believe it's a four-letter F-word: **Fear.** Fear of change. Fear of the unknown. Fear of vulnerability. Fear of asking for help. Fear of failure. Fear of success. Fear of hard work. Fear of what others think. The list can go on and on. If you follow the origins of insecurity, doubt, and worry, you'll find they follow a winding road leading toward fear.

The antidote to fear is courage. However, we cannot display a sense of bravery without some form of a threat, risk, or adversity present. Just like the coward, the warrior feels the fear. Yet, instead of running away, the warrior runs toward the battlefield.

Cornerstone

Multiple leadership and performance experts like Dr. Brené Brown, Brendon Burchard, and Simon Sinek agree that courage and vulnerability are the cornerstones of peak performance. I'm a firm believer, too. Here's an example to demonstrate this.

While gathering research for this book, I conducted a wide range of interviews on the topic of courage and confidence. During one interview, I asked my former teammate and friend Josh, a former professional baseball player, if he'd ever had the yips. *Quick reminder, the yips are a mental block that derails your ability to execute a basic task (like throwing a baseball accurately or chipping in golf). For me, I used to have a form of the yips while trying to speak fluently in a formal setting.*

Josh said that he had the yips once, and in fact, his older brother—a former number one Major League draft pick—did too. Their experiences, however, were much different.

Through help from his coaches and teammates, Josh overcame his inaccurate throws to first base from his shortstop position. He said the change happened when his manager addressed the problem as a group during a team meeting. While gathering the entire team together during spring training on the infield grass one sunny Florida morning, his manager said, "Team, Josh is having some challenges throwing to first base. We are going to love him and encourage him today. We will be more upset if he guides the ball versus letting it rip. We don't care if he sails the ball over the dugout and into the stands. All we care about is that he has the courage to max out his throws and throw with conviction, instead of fear of failure."

Josh said that it was embarrassing and scary at first, but by addressing his problem with his teammates, showing vulnerability, and attacking his fear head-on, he cured his case of the yips by the end of that spring training day.

His brother did not have the same success, and here's why. Josh's brother was a highly touted draft pick who even won an award as the best college baseball player in the country. As a professional, he quickly rose to the Major League level. Several years into his MLB career, he had a hard time throwing the ball back to the pitcher from his position at first base. Instead of asking his coaches or teammates for help, he flew Josh down to spring training early to try to help him fix his case of the yips (without anyone watching). The effort did not prove successful. This mental block an

FEAR
FALSE EVIDENCE APPEARING REAL

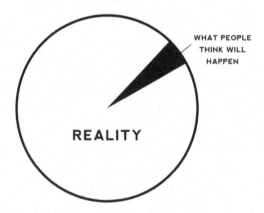

WHAT PEOPLE
THINK WILL
HAPPEN

REALITY

Victory Goes to the Vulnerable

Fear, doubt, and negativity live in the dark. Every day you wait, you add weight to your internal struggle. Don't hold these things in. Shed light on these areas by talking with someone you trust. This person could be a good friend, spouse, teammate, counselor, or coach.

My fluency didn't improve until I finally asked for help and enrolled in speech therapy and later enrolled in a public speaking club called Toastmasters for three years.

One of my favorite quotes on this topic is from NBA mental skills coach, author, music creator, and guest on my Master Your Mindset Podcast, Graham Betchart. He likes to say, "Victory goes to the vulnerable." Yes, so true. The reality is, no one is immune to worry, fear, or adversity. It's part of being human. True courage comes from honesty with oneself and others, and leaning into that discomfort.

The big idea from this section is this: Asking for help is a sign of strength, not weakness. List one person you trust that you can talk to consistently and seek feedback in the area you are looking to improve:

I will speak or meet with that person by (date):

What advice would you give someone you cared about who was going through a similar challenge as you?

What is another area within your life that you feel very confident, comfortable, and perhaps even a level of mastery?

What are examples of your self-talk and actions in this area?

How can you apply this same mindset in the area you want to improve?

ACT: Action Changes Things

It's action time. Think of small, simple actions you can take to slowly practice an activity that you are avoiding, delaying, or are struggling with... or just simply want to improve.

Success doesn't happen overnight. Inner-excellence is not a microwave, but a Crock-Pot®. It's slow cooking.

Another challenge is this fact: **It's the start that stops most people**. Knowing this, start small and simple, then grow and challenge yourself with each step. Break down the act of improving your skills in a specific area in bite size chunks by making a list of eight levels you can advance and progress toward your end goal.

In elevated fear settings, this is called "exposure therapy." Exposing yourself to simpler and smaller steps, then growing to the next challenge once the previous one is completed.

When you start checking off these milestones, you will gain confidence and momentum. This tactic of designing progress through progressive action steps is one of the best ways to generate motivation. Here is a simple example below.

Goal: Run a marathon.

Action steps toward goal:
1. Buy new running shoes.
2. Read articles and interview friends who have completed marathons before and gather stories and advice.
3. Talk to a running coach and create a weekly running plan.
4. Find a running club to join.
5. Begin running three times per week.
6. Increase to running five times per week.
7. Sign up for and complete a half-marathon.
8. Sign up for a full marathon far enough in advance to complete a training plan.
9. Add a date to each step to hold yourself accountable.

I love this concept: What would you do if you knew you couldn't fail? Start by having the courage to take action and to be comfortable being uncomfortable.

Draft your "progress plan" below.

Goal:

Action steps toward goal:

1.

2.

3.

4.

5.

6.

7.

8.

Clearly define your goal and action plan, while understanding that courage comes before confidence. Have the patience and vulnerability to take your "courage to confidence" journey one step at a time. Each time you check one of those steps off your list you will get hits of dopamine, you'll build momentum, and you will feel your excitement grow as you improve your knowledge and skills.

Rewrite your goal here in present tense. Start with the phrase "I am." (Example: *I am a marathon runner who pushes through adversity and is a finisher.*)

Just know that a perfect way to fail a goal is to try to do it perfectly.

How will you celebrate your milestones and improvement? Pick a few nice things you will do for yourself when you progress toward your goal:

Know Fear

I like to help people know fear instead of feel no fear. It's impossible to be fearless. The aim is to fear less. Every human is carrying something or goes through times of worry and doubt. The people who hide tend to stay in a negative state longer. However, if you can **make your mess your message**, talk to someone about what you are going through, and attack your fear, you will obtain an inner-belief that just can't be manufactured any other way. It's supposed to be hard and that's the best part.

That thing you want, but are delaying because of fear, just might be life's best clue to discover your unlimited power.

Here are four final thoughts to close out this chapter:

1. You are not defined by your mistakes, but how you respond to them.
2. If you do what you fear the most, there's nothing you cannot do.
3. God put the best things in life on the other side of fear.
4. When in doubt, ask for help.

In order to grow in this power and develop a quiet mind, you must be open to being vulnerable and failing forward. Now let's learn one of the mothers of all mental skills, **perspective**.

PLAY III
PERSPECTIVE

The brain is remarkable. Those 6-inches between your ears and 3-pound mass made of tissue and neurological connections controls everything in your life.

And with great power comes great responsibility.

This internal power has the ability to either help or hurt your performance. **In other words, your mind can be your biggest strength or weakness in achieving your full potential.** With this concept in place, I hope to shed light on your current perspective and your internal story.

On this topic of perspective, how do you view pressure? It's important to understand that there are two types of pressure that we face in life: *fake pressure* and *real pressure.*

Often we create false stories in our mind to protect our ego, pride, and/ or image. Here's a question to consider: Is your life in danger if someone tells you "no" or doesn't like your performance, outfit, comment, speech, proposal, or Instagram post? The answer is *HELL NO.* We, however, tend to put our self-worth deep into the opinions of others or our perception of what others think. This can be classified as **fake pressure.**

Remember FOPO (Fear of Other People's Opinions)? FOPO is rooted in fake pressure.

Let's break down this fake fear lie in a concept I learned from Jay Shetty, author of *Think Like a Monk*. Speaking on the topic of identity, Shetty shared a 1902 quote written by sociologist Charles Horton Cooley, *"I am not who I think I am. I am not who you think I am.* **I am what I think you think I am."**

THE LIE OF SELF-PERCEPTION

I'M NOT WHO I THINK I AM

I'M NOT WHO OTHER PEOPLE THINK I AM

I AM WHO I THINK OTHER PEOPLE THINK I AM

THIS IS NOT TRUE.

Marinate on that concept for a minute. You are what you THINK other people think you are. I was so guilty of this alarming truth.

It's time to get out of that dark abyss of pleasing everyone and come back to Earth and really focus on what matters. Missing a par putt in golf, losing a business deal, hearing "no," someone not liking your new song, or going through a season of adversity does not define you. Attacking your fears, growing daily, serving others, finding gratitude, being present, and not wasting a day . . . these things are what's most important.

There are nearly 8 billion people on the planet, so why would you let the opinion of one person shape your confidence, self-image, and dictate what actions you take?

WAKE UP! **Just do you!** That mistake you made or negative comment someone said about you is not the real you, but part of a longer journey and story.

Let's practice together. Say these words out loud. These just might be the five most important words you can say as a performer:

"I'M NOT DEFINED BY THIS."

Say it again.

"I'M NOT DEFINED BY THIS."

This applies to failure and success.

Wow—life changing concept, right?

You are a human being choosing to sell a product, perform a task, lead others, participate in sports, parent, create art, star in a play, or contribute to a team. THESE ACTIONS DO NOT DEFINE YOU.

That's the trap I lived in for most of my life. If I had success, I was worthy. If I failed, I was worthless. I spent days, weeks, months, and years consumed by fake pressure wrapped in perfectionism and topped with an obsession of pleasing everyone. My value was tied to "doing" and achieving instead of "being."

But NO MORE!

You will never max out your life with these limiting beliefs. As the saying goes, we are not human "doings," but human "beings." Let your worth flow from who you are, and not what you do.

Now let's examine real pressure.

Real pressure is receiving a late stage cancer diagnosis. Real pressure is not knowing when you'll get your next meal. Real pressure is fighting in a war in which executing your role is a matter of life and death for you and those around you. If you are living through any of these examples, I am extending all of my support and respect to you.

If you are not, remember this phrase: **Pressure is a privilege.**

Not getting likes on your social media post or approval from some random former classmate, teammate, critic, family member, customer, or coworker is not real pressure, but pressure made-up in your mind (aka: fake pressure).

Let's use sports as an example. I guarantee that James Naismith, the inventor of basketball, did not say, "I think I shall invent a game that creates anxiety and fear in people." Not a chance! He created the game of basketball to foster exercise, teamwork, creativity, and explore human potential.

What about a business example? The creators of multilevel marketing (MLM) and direct sales companies did not choose their business models to create fear, self-doubt, FOPO, and crippling comparison syndrome in people who decide to join their business. They developed their products and services to change the lives of their consumers while providing a platform for their builders to earn a phenomenal income and generate lifestyle freedoms unique to most industries.

On the other side of pressure and doing something hard is something amazing. Adversity is an invitation to greatness. No pressure, no diamond. Never in the history of excellence (in any field) have monuments or a statue been constructed in honor of a critic, troll on Twitter, hater or someone who just sits on a couch all day. Nope. Statues and awards are given to honor individuals who attack their fears, leave a legacy, and make things happen.

Legendary American writer John Steinbeck said it best, **"Only mediocrity escapes criticism."**

The Powerful Paradox

Before anybody knew who Marshall Mathers was, he was desperately trying to make a name for himself in the rap scene. While creating his first album, this Detroit native had one goal: make songs that will catch the attention of disk jockeys and get played on the radio. In the mid and late 1990's, there was no iTunes, Spotify or Amazon Music. MTV, BET, and radio were the only places any new hip hop artists could be heard. This radio strategy sounded great in theory, but it backfired in action. Going by the name Eminem, Mathers said this early album was horrible, because he was making music for other people's approval. This killed his creativity and authenticity.

In desperation, needing money, and seeing his opportunities dwindle by the day, he tapped into his brash alter ego, Slim Shady. In this new persona, Mathers found a rebirth. His greatness and legacy came from this revelation—he said "Once I stopped giving a f*ck, people started giving a f*ck."

Wow. When I watched that interview and heard those words, it hit me like a ton of bricks. It's so true. In that moment, everything changed for Eminem. He started writing groundbreaking new songs and winning rap battles with innovative rhyming schemes that were in-your-face and unapologetic. Mathers created a self-deprecating style that no one had seen before (check out Eminem's award winning autobiographical film *8 Mile* for context). His new songs and flows caught the attention of hip-hop mogul Dr. Dre. Eminem signed with Dre's label at Interscope Records and he later became one of the most successful rappers of all-time with multi-Grammy wins and an Oscar award.

The point of this backstory is this: *Everything changed when Eminem stopped being addicted to the approval of others.* In this mental state, his super powers, extreme creativity, and raw authenticity were fully actualized.

Like Eminem, my life, and business for that matter, didn't begin to flourish until I became authentic and vulnerable with my writing, speaking, and messages—whether in person, live events, podcasts, or social media. I still have a long way to go, but there is no other path for me to live.

What about you? Do you allow yourself to be truly yourself? Do you even know who that person is? Or do you spend more time and energy seeking the approval from others and being liked? You will never reach your full potential and develop a quiet mind if your focus is on pleasing others. Your power lies in living in alignment with your mission, gifts, and values... and respectfully not being overly consumed by what others think in the process.

To execute this, the best performers who find lasting success are often able to balance sometimes conflicting characteristics. What if your mindset was conditioned to perform with these dueling traits?

- Confident, yet humble
- Competitive, yet compassionate

- Expert, yet beginner
- Ambitious, yet grounded
- Aware, yet curious
- Determined, yet flexible

Whether it's Beyoncé, Oprah, Justin Timberlake, Stephen Curry, Kristen Bell, Macklemore, Matthew McConaughey, or Mike Trout, these performers (which are a few of my favorites) are able to balance these opposing traits.

I call this mindset the *Powerful Paradox.* Here is the Merriam-Webster Dictionary definition of the word paradox:

1: a statement that is seemingly contradictory or opposed to common sense and yet is perhaps true

2: an argument that apparently derives self-contradictory conclusions by valid deduction from acceptable premises

In simple terms, a paradox is when two opposite forces come together to serve a purpose. In this case, the Powerful Paradox is having the juxtaposition approach of these two concepts: Care/Don't Care.

POWERFUL PARADOX:
CARE/DONT CARE

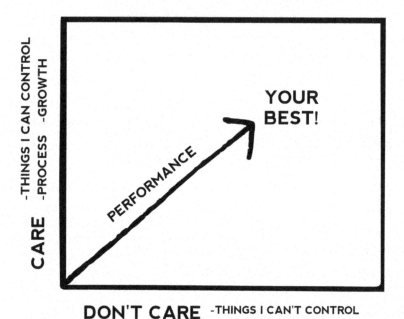

Using this juxtaposed Care/Don't Care model, the aim is to deeply care about your craft, have unwavering self-love and clarity of what matters to you, and sincerely care about the well-being of others. Yet, at the same time do not care or get paralyzed by what others think of you or your actions (or your perception of what others think). Sounds easy and rational on paper, but extremely hard to execute.

Here's why. Being accepted by others is ingrained in our DNA and instincts. Safety, food, and being part of a tribe have essential survival benefits. However, this need to be liked and gain social approval just might be the number one obstacle in developing a quiet mind. It's exhausting trying to fit in and please everyone. I know firsthand. This is one of the biggest challenges that I've worked on my entire adult life. I'm a perfectionist and a pleaser. However, I'm trying to adopt a line from country singer Jo Dee Messina, *"My Give a Damn's Busted"* (which is one of Kendra's favorite quotes).

Question to consider: Why do you care so much about what other people think of you?

This Care/Don't Care mindset has clear benefits in life, performance environments, business, and entrepreneurship. While conducting a regional mindset workshop with a talented group of sales professionals at Rodan + Fields, I asked their upline leader, Sarah Beyersdorf (who is also a dear friend), if she could pinpoint when things really changed in her business. She said without hesitation, "My business and success transformed when I stopped giving a shit about what people think."

Boom. There it is. Author of the worldwide smash and bestseller, *The Subtle Art of Not Giving a F*ck,* Mark Manson sums this concept up perfectly, "Not giving a f*ck doesn't mean being indifferent; it means being comfortable being different."

I love that insight so much.

No one has changed a company, industry, locker room, or community by being like everybody else. I know it often doesn't feel like it, but being unique is a gift to the world.

I'm giving you the permission and freedom to be different. I'm releasing you from perfection. I'm inviting you to explore your true authentic self and let your uniqueness shine bright. Start that journey today. Awaken the giant within and let your voice be heard and your heart be seen. The world needs that person... not a shell of who you truly are. In the words of Eminem:

"You better lose yourself in the music, the moment,
You own it, you better never let it go,
You only get one shot, do not miss your chance to blow,
This opportunity comes once in a lifetime..."

Lose yourself in the real you. Let's build that person together.

What is a unique trait that you can do a better job of optimizing?

Perspective Shift

Aside from the need to shift my perspective on how I see my uniqueness, I often catch myself needing a perspective shift on how I see my environment and circumstances as well. Sometimes I need to adjust my lens back to gratitude and away from worrying about petty things that do not matter in the grand scheme of life.

Here is a way to do just that. Can you think of someone that has either passed away, received a grim diagnosis of some kind, or lives in adverse conditions? This could be an individual and/or a group of people in your community, family, friend circle, your country, or underprivileged parts of the globe.

List that person or group here:

What would they give to have the same opportunities as you?

That might sound a little harsh, but it's true. Because we are on Earth and not in heaven, life-altering events and conditions impact people daily. We often get lost in our own bubble and lose this perspective.

What if you connected with people who are living in adverse or challenging circumstances? How would that shift your perspective?

In my hometown of Seattle, Seahawks quarterback Russell Wilson and his Grammy-winning wife Ciara, visit Seattle Children's Hospital every Tuesday (in person or virtually) during the season to give back, give hope, and share the perspective of love, optimism, and service. This act of kindness not only impacts these patients in a positive way, but it also grounds Russell and Ciara's perspective of what truly matters. During the pandemic, Russell led a campaign to fund millions of meals for people in need. For these efforts, he won the 2021 NFL's Man of the Year Award. When I see leaders like Russ and Ciara provide this type of value I ask, "What can I do to help others in need?" I definitely can get better at this.

Take a moment to reflect.

A person, group, or organization that you plan to visit or serve is:

Just like taking a leap of faith, we also need to **take a leap of service.**

It's Not About You

Being of service to others is a proven strategy to help lower stress, improve health, and activate happy chemicals like dopamine and serotonin. When we are in a funk, we often make everything all about us. **Part of being in a flow state is an exit of self.**

Serving and connecting with others activates the chemical oxytocin, which triggers emotional responses that contribute to relaxation, trust, and psychological stability. Brain oxytocin also appears to reduce stress responses, including anxiety, and is a powerful social bonding chemical.

In moments of acute stress or pressure, revisit your perspective, and most often you will see that your situation is not that bad, and undoubtedly, someone has it much worse. Remember to display empathy for others. **Seek to serve, don't swerve.** Every genuine act of kindness sparks another.

Bloom Where You're Planted

In all kinds of situations, I think of my former college teammate Steve Gleason. After many years in the NFL, he was diagnosed with ALS (Lou Gehrig's disease). Though he received this life-altering diagnosis, and is confined to a wheelchair for the rest of his life, he's still making the most of each day and serving others through his foundation, Team Gleason. With his efforts of raising awareness, funding, and research for those living with ALS, he won the Congressional Medal of Honor in 2019. Wow...so inspiring!

My other go-to person to shift my perspective is the loss of basketball legend Kobe Bryant. Kobe was one of my favorite entertainers of all-time. He had a relentless "Mamba Mentality" that was all about growing daily and becoming the best version of yourself. On that emotional day of loss, we not only lost Kobe in that helicopter accident, but his daughter Gigi and seven other passengers. This was a gut-wrenching reminder and wake-up call for me to not waste a moment and to maximize everything I have.

As part of my mental priming before presentations or new professional environments, I write the number 2437 on my left forearm (Kobe and Steve Gleason's jersey numbers) as a reminder to not take myself too seriously, have a perspective of gratitude, and not waste this opportunity to be of service. This "reset" reminder calms my nerves and helps reframe my situation.

When I'm having a rough day or feel acute stress, I think of Steve and Kobe to shift my perspective back to growing and helping others, instead of protecting my ego. That darn prideful ego. Ego and lack of empathy are the enemy.

Look at this perspective shift: A bad five minutes doesn't mean a bad day. A bad day doesn't mean a bad week. A bad week doesn't mean a bad month. A bad month doesn't mean a bad year. A bad year doesn't mean a bad life.

It's normal to not always have your best stuff each day, feel unmotivated, and notice self-doubt creep in. Challenges and adversity will arise. Dr. Ken Ravizza used to say to the college and Major League Baseball teams he mentored, "Give 100% of what you got. If you only got 70% , then give 100% of that 70%."

Perspective is your greatest ally to do just that. It takes a trained and re-silient mind to have what Ravizza called, "A good shitty day." Blooming where you're planted and being a great teammate is a phenomenal strat-egy to get out of your own way and use the most of what you have, regard-less if you don't have your best stuff.

I'll offer one more "Ravizza-ism" to conclude this section. He used to say, "Are you so bad that you need your A-game to win?" Great point. Gritting out a winning performance isn't always pretty, but being vulnerable, pres-ent, and engaged as possible—especially with those around you—will give you a better chance to find your best and get it done.

I've experienced this truth as a presenter. Some days my confidence isn't there and my words don't seem to come out right. This concept of not needing my A-game, but being able to deliver with my B or even C-game, reminds me to keep competing, keep loving, keep serving, and not make it all about me.

In these moments I have to remind myself, **connection not perfection. And the perfect way to fail a goal is to try and do it perfectly.** In these times I go back to my **2437** perspective reminder. Kobe is no longer here. Gleason is confined to a wheelchair and can't speak—if Steve can demon-strate grit and find a way to deliver in a non-ideal situation—I can step it up and be of service to others too.

I'm more proud of those moments of execution than when everything feels right.

To help you raise your game when you don't feel 100%, let's check in on some perspective and servant leadership questions.

Can you think of a time when you didn't feel your best, but were able to grit out a successful performance? How did you find a way to execute?

How many days in your life do you think you've wasted due to fear or a lack of taking action? Reflect on a moment when you didn't do something because of worrying about what others think of you.

Is there a person or group of people close to you to whom you can do a better job serving?

What do you plan to do to strengthen your service muscle in this area? What acts of kindness will you do for this person or group?

Make the big-time where you are. You have the power to recognize when your perspective is drifting to a prideful fear-based place that does not help you or others. Have a perspective shift ritual and routines like examples shared in this chapter.

In these moments, ask yourself the following questions:
- Is this fake pressure or real pressure?
- What can I learn from this?
- How can I use this adversity to grow bigger, not smaller?
- How can I make this not about me?
- How can I be the best part of someone's day?

In moments of stress, take a deep breath, smile, and say to yourself as many times as necessary: This does not define me. How I respond does.

Then ask yourself: *How can I be of better service to others and myself?*

PLAY IV
PRIMING

I love this quote from a true GOAT (Greatest of All Time), LeBron James, "The mind is like a muscle. The more you train it, the stronger it becomes."

Key mental strength question: When you wake up in the morning, do you focus on who you are or who you aren't? Do you focus on what you have or what you don't have? Do you think about what you want or what you don't want?

Either way, it's time to strengthen how you see yourself and gain clarity on what you want. This is what mental conditioning is all about.

During my mental transformation years ago, I credit a lot of this awakening to my original mindset mentor and sales trainer, Frankie Pretzel. During sales onboarding at Bard Medical, he asked me what my goal was for the year. The only award first year sales professionals in my division could earn was Rookie of the Year, so that's what I told him I wanted.

While driving in his car in the Chicago area and listening to Tony Robbins audios (I spent a week with Frankie in his territory as part of my training), he paused the audio program and told me this, "OK, perfect Collin, that is an awesome goal. Here's the thing, whatever the brain can conceive and believe, it can achieve. As part of your morning routine, visualize every detail of you winning Rookie of the Year. See the hotel, banquet room, what suit you'll be wearing, being called on stage, and giving your speech."

He then concluded, "Do this daily and your brain will find a way to make this vision come true."

And he was right. Thoughts become things after all. I committed to seeing this accomplishment in my mind daily. And guess what? All the things I envisioned would happen, did happen. This priming gave me clarity and motivation to win Rookie of the Year at our National Sales Meeting, even though I was in my role for only 8 months. When I heard my name called and walked on stage, it was an eerie feeling because I had already seen that experience in my mind hundreds of times.

This was a big-time learning moment in my life seeing the power of the mind. I've expanded my priming system (which I'll explain in this chapter) to help me win award trips to Greece, Tahiti, Hawai'i, Bora Bora, Rolex and Tag Heuer watches, President's Club Awards, and now create a business and lifestyle built around using the same power we all have access to—training our brain. I only share this to encourage you to adopt a daily mental conditioning routine as well.

Thank you Frankie for this sage advice.

Clarity is power.

Remember the definition of mindset? Here it is again: **A conditioned set of beliefs that drive behavior.**

What are you doing to condition your mind?

Think about this truth... athletes warm up their bodies before competition, so shouldn't you warm up your mind and spirit before you begin your day? Instead of waking up and scrolling through social media or checking emails first thing in the morning, I've developed a system that will give you much more ROI (return on investment) than comparing yourself to others on Instagram or reading/watching negative news stories.

It's all about **sweat before screen.** Get your physical and mental sweat on, before you stare at a device, screen, or TV.

This system is backed by good science, and it has without a doubt changed my life. It just takes four minutes. Let me teach it to you.

The HAW Method

Before you go to bed or start each day, journal and/or reflect on these prompts:

H.A.W. METHOD

4 MINUTE MENTAL WORKOUT

one minute per step

1. BREATH
2. I HAVE (GRATITUDE)
3. I AM (AFFIRMATIONS)
4. I WILL (INTENTIONS)

I call this the HAW Method. Don't leave your house for the day until you complete this exercise! It will take only a handful of minutes to complete.

Step 1: Breathe

A necessary component of the HAW Method is breathing. Deep cleansing breaths help us become calm and present in the moment. Plus, they feel so good. Take a deep breath right now and see how it makes you feel. While you are breathing, connect to your body. Do a body scan from head to toe and unlock any tension or tightness you may feel. Research shows there are numerous benefits to deep breathing, some of which include lowering stress, improving mood, increasing energy, reducing tension, becoming more present, and improving focus.

Keep these benefits in mind as you progress through the HAW Method.

Step 2: Write Down or Focus on Gratitude

I **Have** statements and thoughts focus on optimism and gratitude.

Research from psychology professor Robert Emmons at the University of California-Davis, shows that a daily gratitude practice significantly reduces the stress hormone cortisol (among many other fantastic benefits) by nearly 30%. Optimism, gratitude, and the act of "savoring," have been proven to increase grit, creativity, health, and overall well-being. Research from the University of Pennsylvania showed that a daily gratitude routine reduced anxiety and even depression.

The foundation of resilience is rooted in gratitude and optimism. Manju Puri and David Robinson, professors of finance at Duke University, found that people who exuded the mental skill of optimism earn more money, work harder, are hired more often, win at sports more regularly, and are more resilient.

Practice this power with the prompts below. Reflect and/or write down what you are grateful for.

People or things that make me happy that I sometimes take for granted:

Personal achievements/accomplishments I am proud of:

Activities that bring me joy:

Events or trips I am looking forward to:

In moments of fear or stress, go back to this list to shift your focus.

Step 3: Write Down and/or Give Yourself Affirmations

I Am statements and thoughts focus on feeding the Good Wolf daily. Do you remember the Good Wolf from the introduction?

While assessing a robust study group of 44,000 people, professor Andrew Lane and the BBC Lab from the United Kingdom found that self-talk was the most powerful tool used to improve confidence and performance.

Daily affirmations are a confidence tool used by greats like Usher, Serena Williams, and Will Smith.

Quick question: Who is your best friend? Would you still be best friends with them if they spoke to you the same way that you speak to yourself? I often ask this question when I'm doing my talks and workshops. The overwhelming answer is "no."

If you said "no" also, it's time to change this bad habit. We produce five million new cells in our body each day. Our cells have memory. These cells are listening to you. Choose your internal and external words wisely, Your language has a direct impact on your inner and outer performance. Are you affirming who you are or who you aren't?

For the sake of practicing being kinder to yourself, take a moment and reflect on your strengths. What unique skills do you possess? In which areas of your life have you had consistent success? Many performance experts believe we grow more in our strengths than in areas in which we are weak.

Build up your confidence. Write down your strengths and/or positive things about yourself here.

Here is a legit quote from Albert Einstein on the importance of embracing your strengths, "Everybody is a genius. But if you judge a fish by its ability to climb a tree, it will live its whole life believing that it's stupid." This ties back into self-awareness. Everyone else is already taken, so you should just be you.

I did this productive self-talk exercise with a Major League Baseball player recently, and it was very difficult for him to write down positie things about himself. His mind was hardwired to remember his mistakes and flaws and not remember or focus on his strengths and/or times of success.

If you are having a similar struggle, it's OK. Even the best performers in the world can improve their self-talk.

Step 4: Identify One Intention

I Will statements give you a purpose and clear goal for the day.

The late Florida State University psychologist Anders Eriksson called this intention setting "deliberate practice," which has been proven to enhance learning, focus, and growth in individuals, far greater than those who do not set an objective for a specific task. Everything happens twice; first in our mind, then in real life.

Write down one thing you want to accomplish today that will help you reach your goal(s) and improve your skills.

Write down one thing you want to accomplish this month that will help you reach your goal(s). This will be a powerful tool to help you assess if you've progressed toward your goal or not.

Next, write down your big goal or goals in present tense as if it is already done. Like my earlier example, I'd write my work awards down as if I'd already won them. Here are some examples:

I'm Rookie of the Year
I'm number one and going to Greece
October = $25K

Write your goals in present tense now:

This exercise of gaining clarity on what you want activates the Reticular Activation System (RAS). The RAS is a cluster of brain cells that helps your subconscious filter out things that do not matter. It's like a heat-seeking missile for your brain to get what it wants. A common example used to explain this phenomenon is when you're looking to buy a new car, you probably see this desired model every time you are out on the road. That's the RAS at work!

Daily Execution

Once you've documented and completed these three areas of focus, (I Have, I Am, I Will) close your eyes, see, and feel these emotions. This mental activity is a form of mindfulness called "visualization." This type of imagery helps create positive thoughts and emotions that lead to more happiness, clarity, and health.

Priming Plan: When and where will you do this daily exercise?

Research shows that selecting a time and place is a critical piece in developing a new habit. Whether you journal and visualize or simply think about gratitude (I Have), affirmations (I Am), and set one clear intention (I Will) for the day, having a consistent routine to take slow deliberate breaths and prime your mindset are powerful tools to set you up for success.

To recap, get your morning mental reps in using the HAW Method (I also call this the "4-Minute Mental Workout").

Journal and/or focus on these four steps:
- **Breathe** (take slow deep breaths for 1 minute).
- **I Have** (focus on gratitude and what you are thankful for, 1 min.)
- **I Am** (practice productive self-talk; feed the Good Wolf for 1 min.)
- **I Will** (set one intention or daily goal and visualize yourself executing that activity, as well as your big dreams for the future, for 1 min.)

This activity will elevate your self-image, improve your mood, invite ideas to find solutions, and create neural pathways for your brain and body to attract success.

PLAY V
POWER OF PROCESS

"Focus on the process, not the prize." – PJ Fleck

While lining up to kick the field goal of his life, New York Giants kicker Lawrence Tynes was facing some tough conditions. Merely seconds remained on the clock during the 2011 NFC Championship Game. The Giants were trailing on the road, in the hostile frozen tundra of Lambeau Field—home of the favored Green Bay Packers. If Tynes made this kick, he would send his team to the Super Bowl. If he missed, their season would be over.

There was a bit of a problem. Earlier in the game, Tynes shanked and missed two field goals, and with the conditions nearing below zero, many wondered if it was even physically possible to make this kick. So, after the Packers called a timeout to "ice" him (literally), Tynes lined up for the kick. He did his measured steps, set his feet, looked up at the holder, and nodded his head. The snap was placed, the kick was up . . . and . . . he drilled it.

The TV commentator yelled, "The Giants are going to the Super Bowl!"

During post-game interviews, reporters asked Tynes what he was thinking before making that kick, especially after badly missing his two previous attempts. Tynes replied that he didn't change a thing. He kept his
focus and poise by sticking to his pre-kick routine.

*When you have to perform in a high pressure situation, do you have a clear
routine?*

Process > Pressure

Nothing happens by accident. The greats in business, sports, military, and
life understand that repeated actions become instinct. By specifying key
actions and routines—and practicing these routines in a variety of settings and conditions—you will naturally create a sense of comfort, calm,
and consistency when it is time to perform.

The human brain burns around 300 to 600 calories per day performing
normal functions. When someone is studying for a rigorous test like the
bar exam or SAT, or in deeply stressful situations, they can burn close
to 1,000 calories. Developing a clear process (as in, mental and physical
disciplines performed consistently) helps lower decision fatigue and con-
serves precious mental energy.

Just to be clear, I'm talking about habits and routines... not superstitions.
Superstitions are beliefs like saying, "If I wear my yellow lucky socks, I'll
have success." This is not a productive strategy. Routines are behaviors
and movements that you master, which will guide your focus. *With superstitions, the power is outside of you. With routines, the power is inside of you.*

For example, one of the most famous peak performance coaches of all-
time, Tony Robbins, always performs the same physical routine before he
goes on stage. He does a quick spin, hits his chest, and says the same affirmation. This "power move" gets him into a peak state and fully switched
on to crush it in front of his live audience or virtual trainings. He even
does a consistent morning ritual as well, where he takes a cold water

plunge and does a breathing, gratitude, and visualization exercise. This "priming" ritual as he calls it, helps him master his "inner-world," which directly influences his "outer-world."

Take time to develop your own routines instead of worrying about outcomes or pressure. You avoid this mental fatigue by building a process plan. Best-selling author of *Drive* and *A Whole New Mind*, Daniel H. Pink, breaks it down beautifully, "Thoughtful design beats willpower."

This chapter is all about helping you design your habits and routines of excellence.

Morning Routine

While researching top performers, I've found that the majority have a consistent and productive morning routine. *Win the morning, win the day.*

One of the first lessons instilled in new Navy SEALs is the importance of making their beds first thing in the morning. This simple act of discipline sets a chain reaction for more successful behaviors to follow throughout the day.

Take a moment to outline what an ideal morning routine would be for you (examples include: hours of sleep clocked, consistent time you will wake up, making your bed, journaling, meditation, exercise, breakfast, etc.):

Consistent Gear

Former President Barack Obama used to wear only blue or gray suits during his presidency. While presenting, Steve Jobs would rock his go-to black turtleneck and jeans. Billionaire entrepreneur and founder of Spanx, Sara Blakely, always brings her trusty red backpack to meetings. MLB postseason hits leader and New York Yankee legend, Derek Jeter, used the same model glove and bat during his entire professional career. Are you seeing a trend?

Build consistency with your performances by clearly defining what tools and gear you will utilize when it's go time. By keeping these consistent, it's one less thing to worry about and this approach will help you not waste precious mental energy on trivial things. My go-to gear when I present or film a video series is a black lululemon shirt and black lululemon ABC pants, with my Nike Air Force 1's. I always have a La Croix handy and my army green Herschel backpack nearby that has all of my stuff (laptop, adapters, dry erase markers, mini Bose sound system, Valor essential oil, handouts, and "reset" bracelets).

I use the same gear even when I present virtually.

A familiar example for this approach is having a consistent spot to put your wallet and keys. If this location is not identified in your home, you are more likely to lose your keys and misplace your wallet. Having a clear spot for these items helps lower your stress and save mental energy, and you go to this location as soon as you need to get in your car and go somewhere.

Your habits and routines work the same way. They will give you a sense of clarity and calm when you have to deliver.

Now it's your turn. List the articles of clothing, specific gear, or tools you will utilize during times of performance. Keep these the same no matter the setting:

Pre-Performance

Let me give you a couple basketball examples of the power of pre-performance routines. Just before LeBron James steps on the court, he goes to the scorer's table and sprinkles white chalk powder on his hands. He then throws the chalk residue in the air. This dials in his mindset, and he feels ready to go after this routine.

Similarly, when he played in the NBA, Kobe Bryant (rest in peace) would untie his shoelaces, then re-tie them just before the start of games. This routine served as a mental reminder to help Kobe get locked-in and awaken his "Mamba Mentality."

Before I present to a group or go on stage, I always get a workout in. I also listen to the same playlist before I speak. If you are wondering what artists I like, you can expect to hear Khalid, Taylor Swift, Justin Bieber, John Legend, Shawn Mendez, and H.E.R. This consistent routine gives me a sense of peace and focus.

What routines do you do leading up to or during the warm-up phase of your performance? Examples: food/hydration, music playlist, writing down affirmations, physical routines, etc. Keep these the same no matter the environment, practice, or pressure situation.

Make a clear checklist here:

Own the Moment

Just before she's about to execute an event, Olympic gold medalist Laurie Hernandez puts her hand on her stomach, takes a slow, deep breath, and says to herself, *"I got this."* Like this example and those of kicker Lawrence Tynes, speaker Tony Robbins, and entrepreneur Sara Blakely:

What routines will you perform directly (as in merely seconds) before you perform your skill (example: taking a deep breath, setting your intention, saying affirmations, looking at one spot in your office or on the field/in the gym, etc.)?

Time Management

We all share the same 168 hours each week. How many days and moments do you waste?

A huge component of owning your process and developing a quiet mind is having a solid daily plan. Are you busy or productive? Do you procrastinate or do you get stuff done? Do you wing it or have structure to your day? Many average performers or people who lack consistency are missing this critical piece to their game.

I picked up this amazing tidbit when working with Jake Jackson, a very successful CEO with Sterling Athletics, who also happens to be a high school basketball coach (I'm blessed to provide mental conditioning support for his team—Go Sumner Spartans!). One day he said, "Eighty percent of my decisions are already made throughout the day."

Wow. Powerful, right? With a hectic work and coaching schedule, while balancing family time, his daily, weekly, monthly, and even yearly plan is the only way he survives.

Let's do an exercise to help you get into the mindset of scaling success. Give your mind the benefit of knowing what a perfect day would look like. In the space below write out your ideal day in three different scenarios in which you are maxing out your actions and productivity:

- **Practice Day** (not seeing clients, customers, or playing a game)
- **Performance Day** (it's go time, you know you will be called to perform in some form or fashion)
- **Off Day** (what does an ideal recovery day look like?)

Here's a brief example for a sales professional.

Practice Day:

6 a.m. - Wake up, workout (sweat before screen), meditate, shower, and eat a solid breakfast.

8 a.m. - Get to my desk and make a list of the top three things I need to accomplish in the day.

8:15 a.m. - Attack the top priority.

9:15 a.m. - Check email for the first time. (If anything is urgent, I would have received a call or text.)

...and so on

Performance Day:

6 a.m. - Wake up, shower, workout, do the HAW Method, and eat a solid breakfast.

7 a.m. - Ensure computer is charged and presentation deck is open and ready to go. Double-check handouts and leave-behind materials.

8 a.m. - Arrive at client's location for presentation.

8:30 a.m. - Scheduled presentation. It's Go Time! Knock it out of the park and expect success. Trust my preparation.

10 a.m. - Leave clients and head to a coffee shop to debrief the presentation.

...and so on.

Off Day:

7 a.m. - Wake up, shower, and eat a solid breakfast.

9 a.m. - Head to the trail for a spirit cleansing hike with friends.

12 p.m. - Lunch after hike.

2 p.m. - Yard work.

5 p.m. - Date night!

Now, it's your turn. Be as specific as possible with times and activities.

Practice Day:

Performance Day:

Off Day:

EPAs

Have you identified what pulls your attention away from being present
and productive? I call this knowing your EPAs, or Energy Pulling Activi-

ties. Multiple sources including *Inc. Magazine* report that the average US employee is productive for only about three hours in an eight hour work day. Why is this? Many reasons: lack of focus, discipline, wasting time on trivial tasks, getting sidetracked, social media, and not being able to concentrate when it really matters.

How productive do you think you are? How many moments do you waste? How often do you get sidetracked?

Don't fall into this trap. Write down three activities that disrupt your focus and productivity (example: social media, text messages, people interrupting your work flow, etc.):

Commit to remove these distractions. I like to call this "addition by subtraction."

Is there a key mindset reminder you can adopt to get your mind back on track when these EPAs pop up?

MITs

I love working with people on maximizing not only their performance, but also their preparation. While coaching a small business owner, together we recognized a gap in his preparation. When making his list of things to do each day (which would sometimes include up to 20 activities), he would feel extreme stress and get caught up on executing tasks that were not vital to his business or could be delegated to someone else. I helped him recognize that he was busy, but not as productive as he could be.

That's when I told him the power of knowing your MITs, or Most Important Tasks. This is the act of identifying the three things that you will do each day, no matter what. It's the concept that if you did nothing else but these three tasks, you'll win the day.

As part of his homework, this leader texted me a picture of his white board in his office that had a spot for his three daily MITs and a picture of a frog (yes, a frog). Inspired by legendary success coach and author, Brian Tracy, I told him it's important to "eat the frog first." Meaning, prioritize completing the hardest task on your list before anything else. This simple morning routine (identify three MITs and his "eat the frog" activity) helped him skyrocket his clarity, execution, and productivity.

Tampa Bay Rays Mental Skills Coach, Justin Su'a, teaches a similar system. He calls this your HIT List—Highly Important Tasks. When I work with sales professionals I sometimes call this list knowing your IPAs, or Income Producing Activities. As in, is what I'm doing right now going to help me grow my business and generate income? If the answer is "no," then don't do it.

Whether you call this checklist your *HIT List, IPAs, MITs, or eat the frog first*, you have two options—you can pick three tasks that you will do everyday without fail, or you can start your day by writing down your three most important actions for that specific day. My client loved this system so much, he taught this process to his entire company. This system proved extra beneficial, especially during the COVID-19 pandemic with many employees working from home.

If you need an example, here is one from my wife, Kendra, who is an award-winning, top-ranking leader in an essential oils company called Young Living.
Below are her daily MITs:

1. Bring value every day on social media.
2. Love on and coach my team members.
3. Follow up and answer my DMs and emails.

This list simplifies her approach and makes her focus crystal clear.

Take time to gain that clarity. In the end, clarity is power. Write down your three MITs:

1.

2.

3.

Yes/No List

Have you mastered the power of "no?" The more successful you become, the more opportunities you will have. Regardless of where you are right now, you will not advance if you say "yes" to everything.

Take a moment to reflect on requests and activities that come up often. Decide which ones either serve or do not serve your mission, vision, and goals.

You will say YES to:

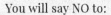
You will say NO to:

Be disciplined enough to execute this plan.

Four Stages of Competency

Excellent job! Developing a consistent process will help lower decision fatigue and help you utilize more mental energy to focus on what's in your control. In the end, the best focus on less, not more.

This plan will also help you develop what's called "unconscious competence," which means you'll have executed these specific movements and tasks so many times, you can do them without thinking (just like tying your shoes or brushing your teeth). Let me further explain *the four stages of competencey*, one of the first mindset tactics that my mindset mentor Frankie introduced me to years ago.

Have you ever heard the expression, "You don't know what you don't know?" This lack of awareness is also called "unconscious incompetence," meaning, you are unaware of crucial information that can help you be at your best. Unconscious incompetence is the state I was operating in for most of my college athletic and young professional career. During my training, I prepared myself physically and honed my craft, but I did not train mentally—largely because I was not taught a framework or process to combat the internal and external noise that arise in moments of performance. Below is a breakdown of these four stages of mastery.

- Stage 1: *Unconscious Incompetence* (I don't know what I don't know).

- Stage 2: *Conscious Incompetence* (I recognize a deficiency).
- Stage 3: *Conscious Competence* (I'm aware and practicing winning behaviors).
- Stage 4: *Unconscious Competence* (I can perform certain tasks without thinking).

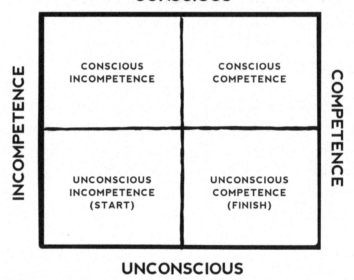

UNCONSCIOUS COMPETENCE

CONSCIOUS

CONSCIOUS INCOMPETENCE	CONSCIOUS COMPETENCE
UNCONSCIOUS INCOMPETENCE (START)	UNCONSCIOUS COMPETENCE (FINISH)

INCOMPETENCE | **COMPETENCE**

UNCONSCIOUS

The goal in performance is to operate in a state of conscious competence that moves to unconscious competence (mentioned above), in which you've rehearsed a specific action so many times that you can perform and execute it without thinking. These repetitions strengthen neurological connections through a process called myelination. Now bare with me, I'm going to get a little scientific here. Myelin is a fatty sheath that covers neurons, which are nerve cells responsible for sending and receiving sensory input. Gray matter is the "outer-shell" of the brain that stores and processes information and emotions. Pathways that connect this gray matter are strengthened via the myelin, which is made up of white matter. White matter helps with communicating electrical impulses to these networks of neurons, including energy chemicals like dopamine, serotonin, and norepinephrine.

This process of "insulating" new neural connections influences neuroplasticity and default behaviors. What's exciting about how the brain functions, is these heavily myelinated neural pathways are up to 300 times faster in optimizing speed and efficiency—kind of like upgrading your Internet connection. Increasing myelination via deliberate practice helps our actions become more automatic. And in turn, the brain will choose the most highly insulated pathways.

This process is like carving a new trail with a machete in the jungle. It takes a great deal of work at first, but each time you come back to that trail and clear the way, that path becomes more visible and easy to follow. These neural pathways are similar.

When I think of this conscious competence to unconscious competence process through myelation, I think of skilled guitar players, ballerina dancers, fly fishermen, chess players, surgeons, or card magicians. With extensive repetitions and muscle memory work, these brain, body, and motor functions become automatic.

In clear terms, the more reps, the more myelin. The more myelin, the more mastery. The more mastery, the less your brain has to work... hence developing a quiet mind.

Let's just make sure that these reps are productive ones that support the right behaviors. You wouldn't want to strengthen mental circuits for bad habits. *What bad mental or physical habits do you need to rewire?*

A simple example of this myelination process is how you drive a car. After driver's education and hours of practice, you don't even think about all of the safety steps necessary to get from Point A to Point B. You've performed these tasks so many times your subconscious mind simply takes over.

Myelin aside, here is a crucial point with this model. Some people skip step three (Conscious Competence) and try to go right into step four (Unconscious Competence). In this instance, they might occasionally find success, but do not know why. These types of performers do well sporadically, but cannot sustain peak performance, because they have no system or process to duplicate. In other words, they are unconsciously competent. While working with leaders, sales professionals, and athletes, I stress the importance of knowing the habits, actions, and routines that they will focus on, so they can replicate their success. That's why one of the first questions I ask my clients is to explain what habits they were doing consistently when they were at their best.

The same goes to you. Do you know the behaviors you must execute to be consistent and confident? Can you perform these skills on command?

According to Stanford psychologist Albert Bandura, the first step of four to improve self-efficacy (a fancy word for *confidence* or *competency in a given skill*) is to do the activity—a lot—and create what he calls "mastery experiences." I call this myelination process "getting your reps in." The other ways Bandura found to improve self-efficacy is through experiencing verbal encouragement from others, learning to control your emotional state, and by vicarious experiences (as in, observing others). A bonus mastery tactic is through visualization.

So, let's do this! Using this framework, know what you want, build your plan, and get your reps in to strengthen myelin and mental pathways. Trust these habits and execute when it matters—all while conserving mental energy.

It's time to reprogram your subconscious mind to help you not hurt you.

Your conscious mind is the goal setter, while your subconscious is the goal getter.

Developing your process is a crucial step toward creating a quiet mind.

List the skills you want to master by getting more reps in that particular area. Using Bandura's model, here's business an example if someone wants to nail their sales pitch or presentation:

1. **Get Your Reps In:** Prepare your outline or slide deck and start practicing it with a variety of people—colleagues, friends, and family.
2. **Verbal Encouragement:** Be in a positive environment where it's safe to fail and grow.
3. **Success Leaves Clues:** Study others who have the skills you want.
4. **Nerves** = **Energy:** Interpret nerves as normal and use them as fuel.
5. **See It In Your Mind:** Have clear intent and visualize success.

By executing these process keys consistently, you will move closer to being in a conscious competent state that will develop into an unconscious competence state.

Build your confidence plan now. Using Bandura's model list how you will do the following...

1. *Get your reps in:*

2. *Put yourself in a positive environment:*

3. *Observe other success people in your craft:*

4. *Better manage nerves (I'll help you with this in the next few chapters):*

5. *Visualize success:*

Coaches and leaders, this is a fantastic model to help your people. Walk them through this framework to help develop their confidence plan.

Remember to focus on progress, not perfection. Instead of "ready, aim, fire," think: "fire, aim, ready." No one is ever completely ready. Have the courage not to be good at first, as well as the patience to keep showing up to improve your craft—that is how mastery is built. *In the early stages, think of quantity, not quality.* Get your reps in, and refine your skills over time to more quality.

Attack this list consistently, develop your process, and build unshakable confidence.

PLAY VI
OPTIMAL PERFORMANCE STATE (OPS)

Have you ever really wanted something, but your nerves got in the way? Let me tell you a powerful story on the importance of developing strategies to use your mind and body to overcome self-doubt, and get into a peak state. This is a real life example of optimizing mental skills to lean into fear and take control of your physiology to execute when it matters most.

Norah's Nerves

While speaking one time at a national sales meeting in the Venetian Hotel in Las Vegas, I had a unique request. As I was about to go on stage and present an hour and a half workshop in front of over 400 sales professionals, Norah, the individual who was going to introduce me, was feeling some serious nerves. While the audio specialist just finished setting up my wireless lapel mic, she asked me for some help.

After pacing for several minutes near the stage, Norah approached me and said, "Collin, this may seem a little random, but, this is my first time speaking in front of this many people. I feel completely nervous. You are a mindset trainer right? So, do you have any tips?"

In all my years as a public speaker I never had this request... as in, right before someone was about to go on stage, they were asking for tips. I was uniquely suited to help though, because I knew exactly what she was feeling.

"Of course!" I said. I used to get so nervous I could hardly speak. I have a few tricks you can use to calm yourself down and improve confidence."

Norah felt a glimmer of hope. "I definitely need that. I have to introduce you in like five minutes, so please coach me up fast!"

With upbeat music bumping and the banquet room starting to fill up with people, I began to give her some tips.

"Alright, you can do this," I said. "I'm going to give you three steps. First, I want you to take several deep breaths—this is called '6-2-8 breathing.' Inhale for six seconds. Hold for two seconds. Exhale for eight seconds. This will take about a minute and help you regain control."

I let her know that fear often induces shallow breathing which activates the sympathetic nervous system of flight, flight, freeze, or hide. Slow, deep breaths helps you get back to the present moment and activates the parasympathetic nervous system which inhibits the body from overworking and restores you to a calm and composed state.

Norah followed her instructions while I guided her first breath, "*Inhale— one . . . two . . . three . . . four . . . five . . . six. Hold—one . . . two. Exhale—one . . . two . . . three . . . four . . . five . . . six . . . seven . . . eight. Alright, now do this on your own.*"

While Norah continued her deep breathing, I chimed in, "Super Bowl-winning quarterback Aaron Rodgers credits deep breathing exercises as his number one pregame routine to gain control of his nerves."

As Norah finished her minute of slow deep breathing, I said, "Nice work. Now, who is the best speaker you've ever heard?"

"Wow, that's a tough one," Norah said. "Uh . . . Brené Brown maybe. I loved her TED Talk on vulnerability."

"Nice! I love her too," I said. "Great example. For the next minute, change your posture and body language to exude confidence and vulnerability just like Dr. Brown. Maybe even pretend that you are her. Walk to the doors of the banquet room and back like you own the place and imagine that people are so excited to hear from you."

While content is king, I also reminded her that a huge source of human communication is not just words, but through body language. A study from UCLA psychologist Albert Mehrabian, showed that 55% of human communication is non-verbal—specifically when talking about feelings and attitudes. Taking this advice, Norah nodded her head and proceeded to walk down to the end of the room and back with extremely confident body language. I briefly told her about research from Dr. Amy Cuddy from Harvard. Dr. Cuddy found that expanding your posture with big body language helps people feel more confident and powerful. Cuddy calls this process "power posing." Your body posture and facial expressions send signals to your brain to release hormones affecting cortisol and testosterone, which influence how you feel and how you act.

Norah listened and practiced using confident and expansive body language one more time. When she returned, I had one final tactic for her to try.

I asked, "Who is your favorite actress of all time?"

"Uh, I used to love watching Julia Roberts movies—still do." Norah shared.

"OK, perfect," I said. "This is the last and most important step. Walk to the doors and back and talk to yourself like you think Julia Roberts would talk to herself. Only use uplifting, positive, and powerful language and see yourself nailing your presentation and introduction."

Norah nodded and followed her instructions and began to walk through the banquet room giving herself positive self-talk and visualizating herself in a confident state.

When she came back, I noticed that Norah's energy seemed completely different.

"All right. Remember this simple fact: Confidence is an action, not a feeling. Nerves are normal and feelings aren't facts—they often lie. You are not going to always feel great before your performance." Then I noted the most important point. I said, "The anticipation is worse than the participation." The trick is to ACT your way into the feeling (just like Julia Roberts) and remember the three steps you just practiced—breathe, act, and think big."

"The anticipation is worse than the participation."

Norah reminded herself those three steps:
1. Breathe big.
2. Act big.
3. Think big.

"Once you get through the first few lines and slide, you'll be just fine and begin to enjoy it. You got this! Oh, and one more thing," I said with a smirk. "No one is worrying about you anyway . . . they are more worried about how they look! Have some fun and try not to take yourself too seriously." Norah smiled and we shared a big high-five.

"I still have some nerves, but I feel so much better. Thank you!"

WHEN YOU FEEL NERVOUS:

BAT BIG

1. BREATH BIG 2. ACT BIG 3.THINK BIG

Norah took these tools and delivered a great opening message and introduction. When we circled back after my presentation, she said she felt butterflies at first, but once she got started and remembered her reminders, she was able to take control of her internal state by owning her breath, body language, and thoughts.

"I'm going to use these tactics again," she said. "The anticipation is definitely worse than the participation. Thank you so much Collin."

As a mindset coach and sales trainer, I was so fired up and proud of Norah's in-the-moment adjustment.

Now it's your turn...

How do you deal with nerves? Do you have a plan to regain control?

I love this perspective shift from World Cup and Olympic champion Megan Rapinoe, "Your opponent is more nervous than you."

"YOUR OPPONENT IS MORE NERVOUS THAN YOU."

— OLYMPIC & WORLD CUP CHAMPION MEGAN RAPINOE

Let's go! Nerves are normal. You too, can master these skills and execute a phenomenal performance. It all starts by getting yourself into a peak state. The rest of the chapter is going to give you more tactics to use your mind to own the moment in the face of fear—just like Norah did.

The Power of Visualization

Successful performers on any stage, like Clay Thompson, Oprah Winfrey, and Jim Carrey implement mindfulness tactics to help take control of their internal state to achieve greatness. They often use visualization or mental imagery to harness the power of their mind to influence their body. These tactics are a phenomenal supplement to your priming exercise (the HAW Method), described in *Play IV: Priming*.

Looking for specifics?

All-time Olympic medal winner Michael Phelps used to spend as much as 30 minutes each day visualizing every aspect of his preparation, including his warm-up, pre-race routines, swimming in the water, overcoming obstacles (like fogged up goggles), winning the race, and celebrating a gold medal. These mental workouts would give him the clarity he needed to dominate.

Mental performance coach and one of my most impactful mentors, Brian Cain, often encourages his Mixed Martial Arts (MMA) clients, including multiple division UFC champion Georges St-Pierre, to practice walking out of the locker room, down the walkway, and into the octagon as if they were about to start their fight. He has them practice their pre-fight routine step-by-step days before their fights—taking control of their breath and self-talk, using big body language, and seeing themselves executing their plan in the cage. When it comes time to actually fight these big matches, his fighters have better control of their focus, physiology, and confidence because they have already practiced their walk-out routine and rehearsed their fight mentally dozens of times.

If these greats and other high achievers use focus techniques and mental imagery as valuable tools to elevate their performance, shouldn't you? These strategies are useful in everyday life as well. Let's learn more.

Mental Imagery

One of my favorite mindset quotes is inspired by the iconic book *Think and Grow Rich*, by Napoleon Hill, "Whatever the mind of man can conceive and believe, it can achieve." Did you know when you imagine your future, the same parts of the brain light up as where memories are stored? In essence, when you take control of your mind and body by visualizing success, you are creating what brain expert and neuroscientist Joe Dispenza calls "a future memory."

Before you are called to execute a specific task (whether in a pressure situation or not), take control of your mind and physiology by using mental imagery. This simple exercise can take seconds or as part of your mental conditioning plan, between five and ten minutes.

Mental imagery is the act of using senses (including sight, sound, smell, feelings, emotions, and focused breathing) to connect with images and physical movements, all while using your mind's eye.

Fun fact: The brain cannot tell the difference between a real or imagined event. Neurons that fire together wire together. By either doing the activity or seeing and feeling yourself doing the activity, you are carving neural pathways that become stronger and stronger with each rep—performed physically or in your mind.

This mental activity is like riding your mountain bike through the same trail. Each trip down and through the trail carves out a smoother and clearer path. Mental imagery work carves out similar neurological paths in your brain (remember myelination from Chapter 5?).

When you visualize yourself performing at your best, you will remember it when that moment comes, and these connections and mental grooves in your subconscious will help you recreate the event you envisioned, and your body will follow. In other words, whether you do an activity physically or in your mind, you are building muscle memory just the same.

Though no mindset expert can guarantee how to get into the zone on command, several high performance psychologists, like Michael Gervais, have documented that utilizing a mindfulness practice like visualization or imagery will greatly increase your likelihood of entering a flow state. If these tactics can help you get even 5% better, I'd say it's worth it!

As explained in the book *The Art of Mental Training*, by D.C. Gonzalez, the soccer great Pelé used a similar technique. Before his matches, dressed in his famous number 10 jersey, game shorts and high socks, Pelé would find a spot in the locker room, roll up a towel, place it behind his head on a bench, lie down, and use imagery in three different time frames:

1. **As a child** when he played for the love of the game on the beaches of Brazil.
2. During **past performances** when he was playing at his best and dominating.
3. **In the match** he was about to play, he would see the crowd and his opponents, and visualize making plays all over the field.

This technique would create a sense of focus and peace for his mindset. Later, he would perform on the soccer field the images he saw in his mind. Moves, passes, and kicks that no one had ever seen before . . . he already made these plays happen mentally, and his body followed.

You, too, can channel this mental power. While working with performers of all types, I often record a custom audio file or voice memo that guides them through this exercise.

Bonus: Listen to music to elevate the experience. Below are the steps to incorporate mental imagery. I call this system **OPS or Optimal Performance State.**

1. **Breathe**: Find somewhere comfortable where you can shut your eyes, be still, and slow down your breathing.
2. **Past Success**: Replay times when you were performing at your best, in a clear state, and experiencing joy. Also, remember when you have overcome challenges and adversity to find success. See and feel these moments of past peak performance.
3. **Future Success:** Make a mental movie and dress rehearse your upcoming performance in your mind. Picture yourself executing at your highest level. Use all of your senses and put yourself in that scene— what you can see, smell, feel, taste, and what you are wearing. Make your own future highlight reel with as much vivid detail as possible
4. **Anchor Your Success:** Just as an anchor keeps a ship at sea grounded

during wind, waves, and storms, create anchor statements to shut up the Bad Wolf and quiet storms in your mind. You do this by mastering your self-talk. List and focus on three neutral or positive thoughts that you will repeat to yourself throughout the day or performance (examples: *I am a competitor. . . . I'm built for this. . . . Trust my training. . . . There's no one like me. . . . I'm unstoppable*).

O.P.S.

OPTIMAL PERFORMANCE STATE

---

1. SLOW YOUR BREATHING

2. REPLAY PAST SUCCESS

3. VISUALIZE FUTURE SUCCESS

4. ANCHOR STATEMENTS

EVERYTHING HAPPENS TWICE -
FIRST IN OUR MIND, THEN IN REAL LIFE.

Former MLB All-Star pitcher turned mental skills coach, Bob Tewksbury (who works with the Chicago Cubs and is the author of *Ninety Percent Mental*), teaches this "anchor statement" system. He says that this self-talk technique helps quiet your inner-critic.

Here's an anchor statement example from one of my best friends since childhood, Jason Johnson. Jason left the University of Arizona as the all-time passing leader at the quarterback position. He later had a stint in the NFL, won a Grey Cup championship in the Canadian Football League (CFL), and while playing professionally in Europe, Jason won multiple titles as well. Before each game this was his anchor statement routine to get into the right headspace and create confidence… he would say to himself, "*I always play good.*"

He said this was his simple way to shape his self-talk and belief—to as he put it—"Trust and talk myself into success."

Man, when he shared this with me during my *Quiet Mind* interview with him, it got me so fired up. Maybe that's because this was the opposite of how I used to talk to myself. Upon learning this from Jason (aka J-Twice as I like to call him) I said this affirmation out loud several times just to see how it felt. There was something in that phrasing that was just reassuring and encouraging. I felt more confident every time I said it.

Jason is now making big plays off the field with this affirming mindset. He is now a two-time Emmy-Award winning filmmaker and he uses that same mantra before big shoots with clients like ESPN and CBS Sports, or producing interviews with titans like Barack Obama, DK Metcalf, and Martha Stewart. Check him out at jasonryancreative.com.

Try saying this out loud yourself:

I ALWAYS PLAY GOOD.

If you don't like the word "play," insert whatever verb is applicable to you and your craft. *I ALWAYS sell, sing, dance, listen, present, film, act, create, cook, perform GOOD.*

Either way, always remember, it's crucial to focus on who you are, not who you aren't. Decide who that person is. See it. Speak it. Then be it.

Brain coach and rapid learning expert, Jim Kwik, agrees that your inner-voice is critical to optimal performance. He says, "Your brain is a super computer and your self-talk is a program that it will run." Upgrade your self-talk... upgrade your life.

Now it's your turn. Make your list of anchor statements here. What are three power statements you will say to yourself to anchor your performance?

This is yet another example of thought replacement. Remember, you can only focus on one thought at a time. Do you recall when I mentioned the power of building your internal advertising campaign? Well, now is your chance. **Train your mind not to listen to yourself, but talk to yourself.** Your mind will naturally go negative if you let it wander. Stop this pattern. No one has more influence over you than you do.

When and where will you utilize this imagery and self-talk system as part of your daily routine?

What song or playlist will you use to help you reach a peak state during your preparation? (My go-to song pre-performance is OTW, by Khalid)

Below are two studies I often reference on the power of imagery and mental rehearsal.

Free Throw Accuracy

A study conducted by sports psychologist Dr. Judd Biasiotto at the University of Chicago showed the power of imagery. He gathered individuals and split them into three groups and tested each group on how many free throws they could make. After this, he had the first group practice free throws every day for an hour. The second group didn't physically shoot, but would simply visualize themselves making free throws. The third group did not shoot or visualize.

After 30 days, he tested them again. As expected, by doing nothing, the third group did not improve their free throw percentage. The first group, that practiced shooting at the gym, improved accuracy by 24%. And what is astonishing, the second group that simply visualized, improved their accuracy by 23% without touching a basketball! This study made a powerful point that by using imagery, you can improve your skills.

Mental Workouts

The Cleveland Clinic Foundation exercise psychologist Guang Yue studied and compared people who worked out at a gym versus people who did virtual workouts mentally. He found a 30% muscle increase in the group that went to the gym and lifted weights. What's fascinating is the second group didn't physically lift weights, but simply used that time to visualize lifting the weights. This group who didn't lift a single ounce physically, but used their mind to lift weight mentally, increased muscle strength by almost half as much, at 13.5%. This average remained for three months following the mental training, showing it's possible you can make your muscles stronger with your brain!

These are just two studies of many showing the science is clear: train your brain, conserve physical fatigue, and improve performance by getting your mental reps in.

Your State Influences Your Self-Image

Using a framework like this will naturally elevate a powerful element that controls your success—your self-image. Automatically, you have an image of yourself, and you tend to act accordingly. By reprogramming your mind to focus on gratitude, successful times, using positive self-talk, and visualizing your future self crushing it, you are creating future memories. You will begin to act as the person you see and want to become. How you see yourself is how you function, and you cannot act consistently otherwise.

Quality Thought = Quality Movement

Negative Thought = Negative Movement

It basically comes down to how you see yourself, which influences your internal and external communication, which directly impacts not only your performance, but your life. Take a moment to reflect. How do you talk...

- About yourself to yourself?
- About others to yourself?
- To others about yourself?
- To others about others?

Apple founder Steve Jobs once said, "Don't let the opinions of others drown out your own inner-voice."

Do you currently have a common negative thought or negative label of yourself? For example: I'm never clutch or I'll always be out of shape.

It's time to unlearn these limiting beliefs and rewire a more productive inner-dialogue and image of yourself.

Pay close attention to these fundamental laws of success: If you think you can, or you can't, you are right. Similarly, if you think you are, or you aren't, you are right as well. We spend all our life studying others, but not ourselves. It's time to destroy old negative thought patterns and rewrite a new, more positive one. We will talk more about elevating your self-image in Play X: Become Limitless.

5-10 Second OPS

Now I'm going to teach you an imagery and mental toughness system that can be implemented in the heat of the moment (just like the example of me coaching Norah at the beginning of the chapter or when negative thoughts pop up like the ones you just listed above). Remember, awareness precedes behavior change. To recover from failure or doubt, use a shorter version of this strategy to activate an Optimal Performance State.

One of my dear friends, Kali Gesser, was an all-conference Pac-12 volleyball player and is now a successful pharmaceutical sales professional and mom of three. She uses a similar technique. During one of my interviews with her, she shared how when she noticed fear pop up, or if she had a string of unforced errors as a setter, she would quickly remember some of her best passes, sets, and performances. Then she would be intentional with her self-talk to get her mind back on track—all in a matter of seconds.

"That approach of quickly replaying times of past success was so crucial to my performance and kept me from turning one or two bad plays into five or six," she told me. "I even use this quick mental approach in my sales career and as a mom."

I love this. You can use this quick reset strategy in all facets of life.

To review, when you feel your biochemistry elevating due to doubt or worry, below are the steps to execute your quick OPS plan:

1. **Body and Breath:** Slow down and get yourself back to center by taking one or two deep breaths while practicing big body language.

2. **Past Success:** Remind yourself of a moment of prior success.
3. **Mental Movie:** See yourself executing your goal and achieving future success (making a shot, nailing your sales pitch or speech).
4. **Anchor Statements:** Say one to three anchor statements to influence confidence.

Taking control of your internal state is one of the most important elements of maintaining a quiet mind (I'll give you more tools on how to do this and "Reset" in Chapter 8).

During times of performance, are you in a *thrive* or *survive* mode? Being confident and composed can be trained. It all comes down to owning your biochemistry. Take 10 seconds and give this technique a try right now: Take a deep breath; remember a time of past success; visualize yourself executing your next attempt; and give yourself positive self-talk on repeat. In essence: BREATHE, ACT, and THINK BIG!

Nerves in a performance setting are like waves in the ocean... they are going to come in and out whether we like it or not. Like the ocean, some waves are big, while some waves are small. The key is to not fight or avoid the waves, but to learn how to surf these waves and allow them to guide you to peak performance.

By upgrading your thoughts, routines, and self-concept through imagery, you will take control of your state and use that momentum to ride the wave toward the best version of you. So, if your energy is like the ocean waves, then this OPS system is like your surfboard—it will guide you to use the moving current of the moment—and give you the best chance to get to flow. So grab your board... it's time to surf!

PLAY VII
FRAME YOUR FOCUS

When I think of getting in the zone, my mind immediately turns to a scene from the old school movie *For Love of the Game*, starring Kevin Costner. Whether or not you're into sports movies or even sports references, the theme of the scene is applicable to quieting whatever noise is distracting you.

Costner's character, Billy Chapel, is a veteran Major League pitcher for the Detroit Tigers. In this particular scene, he's standing on the pitcher's mound in the hostile Yankee Stadium as fans are screaming, trying to distract him. He looks to the crowd and clearly hears the following jabs in a New York accent: "You suck!" . . . "You couldn't pitch a tent!" It's almost like every single sound is amplified as he prepares for his first pitch.

Then, the crowd blurs as Chapel prepares to throw his first pitch, and he says to himself, *Clear the mechanism*. All of a sudden it's like someone hit the mute button. He's unfazed and completely focused. All of the noise and distractions are blurred out and silent. With this focus trigger he hones in on his target and pitches a strike.

Do you have a focus trigger like this? The on-demand ability to quiet the noise and focus on what you want to execute? Elite concentration precedes flow.

I've said this before, but it's worth repeating: **The best focus on less not more.** When people are performing below their abilities, it's often an issue of focusing on too many things or the wrong things.

Energy flows where focus goes.

A trained mind is a focused mind.

Just like every other tactic in this book, you can train your mind to blur the crowd, silence the haters, and lock-in on whatever it is that needs your undivided attention. It's time to starve your distractions and feed your focus.

FRAME YOUR FOCUS

IN MY CONTROL

OUT OF MY CONTROL

To help you frame your focus, below are a few exercises to improve concentration.

Cannot Control

People get off track sometimes because they major in minor things. They let little distractions snowball into big problems. I used to be an expert at that—judging and critiquing my every step. I would judge my performance from the **outside-in** (what I thought people would see, which is out of my control) versus **inside-out** (what I see and experience, which is in my control). I used to spend all my time thinking about what other people were thinking. This is not the best strategy for success.

If I were to ask you to write down all the things in your life that cause you stress, I'd wager that when you broke them all down, a majority of that list are things that are out of your control. To help avoid this trap, make a list of people, factors, and things that you **cannot control.**

Stop worrying and giving your energy to these distractions (examples: other people's opinions, your competition, the weather, umpire/referee, outcomes, your past, your boss, etc.).

List your top triggers that you cannot control that sabotage your focus and drain your mental energy:

Let's be aware of this list and stop performing from the outside-in, but train our mind to execute from the inside-out. Here is a mental drill on how to do just that.

Can Control

Instead of wasting your mental energy focusing on factors you cannot control, make a list of things that you **can control** (effort, self-talk, executing routines, breathing, etc.). By focusing on these controllables, you will lower your stress and increase your likelihood of just being yourself and performing at your best.

Take a moment and write down things that you can control. I call this "framing your focus." List as many as you can think of:

Just like jockeys use "horse-blinders" to keep their racehorse focused on what's in front of them and avoid distractions, use this list to *"stay in your frame"* and lock-in on key thoughts and behaviors to perform at your best.

Box Breathing

Boats do not sink from water that is outside the boat. Boats sink when the water gets inside the boat. A loud mind versus a quiet mind is very similar. If there is a leak of negativity that is continually infiltrating your thought life, it has the potential to wreck your performance.

To help you train your mind to be quiet and block out distractions, I want to dig deeper and teach you a concentration technique I call "Frame Your Focus." This is the practice of mentally tracing a box with your breath. You might be thinking: *Why and how would I do that?* Well, I'm going to take you step-by-step through this technique. The neutral act of framing a shape mentally will help you build a fortress for your focus and block out thoughts that do not support your precious brain space.

Many sport psychologists, including Colleen Hacker, who has coached several USA Olympic teams including women's soccer and field hockey, teach this technique, which is often called "box breathing." There are four parts to the breathe: the inhale, hold, exhale, and hold. Most mental performance coaches who coach box breathing have you trace the box in those four steps counting to four or five each step. My method is a little different. I don't like holding my breath that long. I'll show you my method.

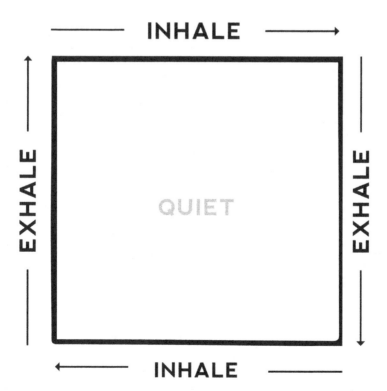

Frame Your Focus Steps:

1. **Picture a box, rectangle, or square in your mind.**
2. **Trace each side of this shape with your breath.** With your inhale, breathe in and trace the bottom of the box from right to left. With your exhale, trace the left side of the box from bottom to top while you breathe out. With your inhale, trace the top line of the box from left to right. Finally, trace down the right side as you breathe out again.
3. **Continue this exercise as long as necessary.**

If you'd like to add another layer to this exercise, try this.

Once you've turned down the volume in your mind by tracing a box several times, count to ten with your breath. With each exhale, see a number inside the box. For example, for your first rep, you would exhale and see the number 1 inside your square. On your second exhale, you'd picture the number 2, and so on.

I use this technique to help me fall back asleep when I wake up in the middle of the night, or if I catch my internal activation elevating due to nerves. This strategy and practice reminds me to slow down my breathing, become more present, and block out thoughts that are unproductive or distracting. This technique helps me slow down my mind and be more calm.

Give it a try. Stop what you are doing right now and practice framing a box shape with your breath.

MSNBC

Looking for another tactic? The cool thing about peak performance is everyone is different and can use a variety of systems to regain focus and control. One of the first strategies I learned in speech therapy was how to calm my nerves through slow deep breathing and flexing and relaxing my muscles. From the book *Positive Intelligence,* author Shirzad Charmine offers a sensory technique of using touch to help calm down and stay present. Three-time Gold Glove winner and MLB All-Star, Evan Longoria, looks at the left-field foul pole to reset his mind. Volleyball and tennis players do a pre-serve routine to improve effectiveness and lower nerves before they hit the ball.

University of Pittsburgh neuroscientists Dr. David Rabin and Dr. Greg Siegle developed a wearable device called Apollo Neuro that produces low frequency inaudible sound waves you can feel, but can't hear. These vibrations have been clinically proven to improve your body's stress response, focus, heart rate variability (HRV), sleep, and overall recovery. All of these examples I just shared prove there is no one way to quiet your mind, calm nerves, and elevate resiliency skills.

Paddy Steinfort knows all about training resilience and mental toughness. Steinfort, who was once a professional Aussie Rules football player, left Australia to earn his masters degree in performance psychology at the University of Pennsylvania. He is now the Director of Mental Performance with Australian Football (American Soccer). Steinfort has worked with organizations like the Toronto Blue Jays, Boston Red Sox, Philadelphia 76ers, Philadelphia Eagles, Texas Tech Red Raiders, military groups, and business executives. He stresses the importance of "psychological flexibility." While being trained by well-known Penn psychologist and best-selling author, Dr. Angela Duckworth, Steinfort offers a focus system he calls **MSNBC**. This is not the cable news channel, but a list of different techniques you can use to lower nerves and stay in the present moment. Let's break this MSNBC system down.

M - Movement: Focus on using your body, motion, and physical routines to quiet the noise.

S - Sight: Look at a spot, focal point, image, visual cue, or maybe even words to read (Paddy helped one of his NBA players manage pregame jitters by reading the words on banners hanging in the rafters).

N - Noise: Focus all your attention to a sound (specific noise around you, music, or external self-talk).

B - Breath: Shift your attention to your inhale and exhale.

C - Contact: Use your sense of touch to shift your focus (touch a garment, piece of gear, equipment, or feel the contact of your shoes or feet on the ground).

Take a moment and practice all five of these focus strategies one at a time: **Movement, Sight, Noise, Breath, and Contact.** These examples will help block out unproductive thoughts and influence staying calm and neutral.

Can you think of a good time to use these techniques to better manage a stress trigger?

Which of these MSNBC strategies is your favorite that you'll use the most?

Coaches, teachers, or business leaders, when would be a good time to practice these strategies with your team?

Focus Keys

Now that you've developed a system to help concentrate on what's in your control and block out external and internal noise by framing your focus and/or using a MSNBC technique, I'd like to introduce you to another tool that will help you quiet your mind. It's all about identifying your focus keys. Clearly identifying the specific actions you'd like to perform during the execution phase of your performance will help you simplify your overall thought process. This clarity is like shaping a key or selecting the digits necessary to open a padlock. This clarity will provide steps to open consistent high performance and unlock your best.

As told in mental conditioning coach Trevor Moawad's book, *It Takes What It Takes*, former Olympic great and world record holder Michael Johnson compared not having a performance plan like going to the grocery store without a shopping list. You might feel inefficient, cluttered, and easily distracted. Before each race (including his record-breaking, multiple gold medal-winning performance in the 1996 Olympic Games in Atlanta) he would write down and focus on his focus keys. Johnson's keys were:

1. Head down
2. Pump my arms
3. Explode
4. I'm a bullet

During stressful performance moments, Johnson would quiet the noise by focusing on those keys.

The brain can only focus on one image at a time. This cognitive substitution technique of training your mind to focus on neutral or productive thoughts versus letting fear-based thoughts sabotage your performance, is a much more effective strategy.

In other words, instead of letting your brain ruin your performance with *stinkin' thinkin'*, focus on *shrinkin' thinkin'*—as in, shrink what you focus on. Less is best.

Write down three focus keys below and train your mind to focus on the function (in your control) and not the future (out of your control). This list is what you will focus on right before and during your performance.

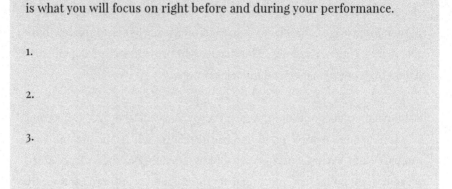

1.

2.

3.

My focus keys before a presentation are:

1. **Joy** - remember to have fun, be myself, exude enthusiasm, and savor the moment
1. **Faith** - trust my experience, knowledge preparation, and believe (I can do all things through Christ who strengthens me. -Phil 4:13)
1. **Love** - serve the audience with gratitude, devotion, compassion, and an unwavering love for their well-being

This helps me quiet the noise and focus on what truly matters.

Let's do this! Stop judging your performance on just outcomes. Instead, judge yourself on your internal state. Reflect, amidst the chaos, *was I able to get to a place of calm and clarity? Was I able to execute my focus keys?*

Concentrate on this checklist before each rep or performance instead of thinking about your past, what could go wrong in the future, or what is out of your control. This strategy will help you to focus on the process, not the pressure.

Intention

In this book I've offered many sports examples, but let's focus on business now. While coaching sales professionals, entrepreneurs, speakers, and leaders on preparing for their presentation, I remind them, "Instead of thinking about what you don't want to have happen, identify your intention and focus on what you do want to have happen." I will often say, "Shift your attention to your intention," and visualize it first.

I remind them to be flexible on how they achieve their goal (there are often many variables that arise during the act of a sales call or meeting), but never to walk into an interaction without this intention:

- Stating what your objective is
- Focusing on service and abundance, not on scarcity
- Detaching your worth from the outcome
- Walking through the call in your mind first

In the military, they call this "commander's intent"—clearly identifying the purpose of the mission. It's crazy just how many calls sales professionals waste because they have no plan, no intention, they just wing it, or they focus on what they don't want. This pre-meeting imagery takes only a handful of seconds and has been proven to work in other performance settings as well.

I ask sales professionals and presenters to set an intention on their goal for the interaction and base that plan on the following questions:

1. **How am I going to show up?** (This includes the specific traits you wish to exude like high energy, empathy, listening intently, etc.)
1. **What do I want to learn?** (What questions will I ask to better understand their needs and challenges?)
1. **How will I bring value?** (It's all about service, not selling)

This framework will simplify your approach and provide direction and clarity for your interactions. These three questions were inspired from a TEDx talk by Andrew Horn. Horn, who once suffered from social anxiety and feared he would never be a successful entrepreneur because of his fear of public speaking. Answering simple questions like these before speaking helped him overcome his fears to create what he calls "social flow."

Intention setting isn't just for business professionals. It's for everyone and can be tweaked to fit whatever you are doing. While working with golfers, I encourage them to set a clear vision with their performance. I tell them to hit every shot three times:

1. Once before each swing mentally.
2. Once physically (actually hitting the shot).
3. Once replaying how they wanted to see that shot perfectly and feel it physically.

This approach seemed to work for all-time golf great Jack Nicklaus. This 18-time major champion said he never took a shot before seeing it in his mind first.

"I never hit a shot, even in practice, without having a very sharp, in focus picture of it in my head. It's like a color movie. First I 'see' the ball where I want it to finish, nice and white and sitting up high on the bright green grass. Then the scene quickly changes and I 'see' the ball going there: its path, trajectory, and shape, even its behavior on landing."

Nicklaus also said, "I never miss a putt in my mind." I love learning insights like this—especially from greats like Nicklaus who understand the power of avoiding mental negativity by visualizing success first.

I'm always looking for examples to teach the power of having a clear vision. One of my favorite movies is *The Patriot*, starring Mel Gibson. During the violence of the Revolutionary War, Gibson's character teaches his sons this focus key, "aim small, miss small." The point is this: If your target is narrow and clear, even if you miss when you shoot, you'll have a better chance of getting the job done.

The same can be said with your performance keys, focus, and vision. If you set low, easy goals and hit them . . . well, big deal. Imagine me doing a patronizing slow clap. I'd rather see you set high goals, go for them, and maybe you just miss. Now envision me giving you a big high-five and yelling "Let's Go!" Peak performance expert Steven Kotler notes that setting a high hard goal is one of the most effective strategies to activate creativity and motivation.

In closing, Earl Nightingale said it best, "You become what you think about most of the time, and that's the strangest secret." To me, there is no secret, but it is quite obvious. Never forget that in performance and in life, **what you focus on you will find.**

This is a fundamental law of success. Train your mind to focus on what you want, not what you don't want.

In the next chapter I'll discuss how to respond when faced with adversity along this path to greatness and high performance.

PLAY VIII
RESET

Most of this book is full of reflective questions with simple tips and strategies. This chapter is a little different. If you ask me what is the most essential trait that separates top performers from the rest, it's simple. It's their ability to overcome setbacks and adversity. These high achievers use challenges to not stop them, but fuel them forward. The mental skill of resilience and fortitude is so important to me, I wanted to give you real life stories and examples of this mindset in action.

Resilience in fact, is the number one trait I hope my children develop (generosity and confidence are a close second and third... in case you are wondering). I hope the stories I share in this chapter inspire you to persevere no matter what challenges you face. So sit back, relax, and take a moment to learn real life examples of what University of Pennsylvania psychologist, Angela Duckworth, identities as the number one predictor of success—GRIT.

If you follow college hoops, you likely know the 2019 NCAA men's basketball champions celebrated more than a victorious season when they cut down the nets. Standing on stage receiving their trophy, the University of Virginia Cavaliers wrote a story of redemption. Just one year prior to their championship, Virginia headed into the tournament as the number one overall seed and lost its first game to a number 16 seed. This wasn't just an embarrassing loss. It was the first time in history a top seed lost to a 16 seed.

The loss is something head coach Tony Bennett said "refined" his program. I had the privilege of spending some time with Coach Bennett, while we both worked at Washington State University. I was hurting for him and his team as well.

In an interview with best-selling author and one of my favorite leadership authors, Jon Gordon, Bennett said, "When you fail miserably, especially, it humbles you and it's painful. But, in that process, I think it's good because it draws you to what truly matters."

Bennett used the loss to teach his players about the importance of learning through challenges and owning setbacks. He also credited his wife Laurel for helping change the trajectory of his thoughts about failure.

"About two weeks after we lost, she said something to me: 'This might not make sense to you, but you are kind of worthy to suffer and to be faithful to what matters to you. That's a privilege. To suffer and fail but still remain faithful to the things that are important to you and to your program.'"

Bennett said his wife also encouraged him to watch a TED Talk given by storyteller Donald Davis, filmed in the same town as the University of Virginia. Bennett took a line from that talk that became what he called a "rallying point" for his team. Here's the line:

"You must learn that it is never tragic when something people think is bad happens to you. Because if you can learn to use it right, it can buy you a ticket to a place you would never have gone any other way."

Their epic fall, then rise to National Champions the following year, is one of the most redemptive stories sports has ever seen. What would have happened had the Cavaliers not suffered that historic loss? We will never know, but one thing's for sure, Coach Bennett and his staff didn't crumble because of adversity. They used the lesson as a cornerstone for building a stronger foundation for their program, one clearly strong enough to soar to the greatest heights possible for a collegiate team.

I bet you're a little curious about that TED Talk Bennett referenced, am I right? You probably haven't heard of Donald Davis or his father, Joe Davis, but if you watch this 2014 TEDx Talk, you likely won't forget him anytime soon (you can find it on YouTube... search, "How the story transforms the teller"). Donald Davis is a professional storyteller, and in this particular feature, he speaks about his father whose name was so common he was one of three Joe Davises in the small town where he lived. Each Joe Davis was known by his profession, and Donald's dad was "Joe the Banker."

One evening as a young boy, Donald was at his dad's bank and closed up shop with him, when a furniture store owner across the street simultaneously locked his doors. The two adults waved and said goodnight to each other, except instead of calling Donald's dad "Banker Joe" or even just "Joe," the furniture store owner said, "Cripple Joe, you have a good night, too."

Once Donald got into the car with his dad, he mentioned how he did not like how the furniture store owner called his dad "Cripple Joe" when he was supposed to be "Banker Joe." Instead of just heading home, Joe decided to tell Donald a story from his childhood—a story his mother made him tell over and over again so that he would understand what he, and everyone involved in the ordeal, learned from it.

Joe grew up on a farm as the eighth of 13 children (*wow!*). When he was just five years old, he saw his father and two of his older siblings cutting shingles for a new roof, and he wanted to help. When the rest of the family went into the house for dinner, Joe stayed outside to touch all the tools he was asked to stay away from. He started chopping things left and right, and just before he planned to head inside, he went to return the axe and ended up chopping through his leg. Sparing you the gory details, Donald's parents rushed him to a doctor who said Joe's leg would need to be amputated. Not accepting that prognosis, Joe's parents traveled 172 miles by train to Atlanta where a brand new hospital had just opened. Doctors were able to save his leg, but he was indeed handicapped because of the injury.

Joe continued his story and shared how he was not physically able to do the manual farm labor like his brothers, so he took up sewing and the chores the women typically did. As he got older, he knew he needed to find a living that didn't involve physical labor, so he decided to go to business school. He didn't even have enough money to cover one term, but he was so determined that he asked if he could attend until the money ran out. In less than one term, he learned all of the skills the program typically taught over the course of two years.

Joe's life took another turn when his father passed away the following year, leaving Joe to help raise his younger siblings, help care for a live-in aunt, and assist his mother. He said for the next 20 years of his life, he raised kids, worked, and saved money. He worked so hard he didn't even think of marriage. At the age of 41, a man who started a bank in his town decided to sell and because he had been saving for decades, Joe became the new bank owner. Three years later, he met his wife.

In the car Joe said to his son, "Don't you get it? If I hadn't gotten to be Cripple Joe, I would never have gotten to be Banker Joe." He continued (with the line that Tony Bennett used all year to inspire his team), "You must learn that it is never tragic when something people think is bad happens to you. Because if you can learn to use it right, it can buy you a ticket to a place you would never have gone any other way."

I encourage you to read that quote just one more time and really reflect on its meaning. Can you think of "bad" things that have happened in your life? What great things transpired or unique paths have you traveled because of these experiences?

Here's the last redemptive story for you, unrelated to the previous two.

I mentioned her briefly before, but Sara Blakely is one of the wealthiest self-made women in the world and one of my favorite entrepreneurs to learn from. If you don't know who she is, just Google "Spanx" to see the mega-brand that began when Blakely couldn't find the right undergarment to wear beneath a pair of white pants. If you dive into her story, you'll find this girl has tenacity and grit, and she made her dreams come true through determination.

When Blakely came up with the idea for the first Spanx undergarment, she knew nothing about fashion design, let alone hosiery, but she believed in her invention. Also, by this point in her life, she'd collected a lifetime of failures selling fax machines door to door, which gave her the confidence to relentlessly pursue success. In countless interviews, Blakely credits her father who would ask her and her brother one question every day after school. This wasn't the typical question most parents ask like, *How was your day? What did you do? What did you learn?*

Nope. The question that shaped this business mogul's mindset was this, "Did you fail today?"

ASK YOURSELF THIS DAILY:

"DID I FAIL TODAY?"

IF YOUR ANSWER IS NO, YOU ARE NOT GROWING.

Sara often shares that if she or her brother would say "no" their dad would challenge them to get out of their comfort zones and try something new. She said her dad would always make them feel proud of their effort.

In a *Business Insider* interview, Blakely said, "What it did was reframe my definition of failure. Failure for me became not trying, versus the outcome."

If Sara Blakely would have listened to all the voices who said her invention wouldn't work or crumbled at any of the numerous roadblocks or setbacks she encountered on her journey, she never would have developed her invention. I'm sure she felt discouraged along the way, but each challenge propelled her to follow through.

I tell you the stories of the UVA basketball team, Joe the Banker, and Sara Blakely because it simply doesn't matter whether you're an athlete, stay at home mom, teacher, or a business professional—failure is a part of life. No one is immune to setbacks and challenges, especially on the road to greatness. It's all about how you reframe your mindset and harness the lessons from those failures to propel you instead of pull you into a pit of angst or downward spiral.

Circling back to grit expert Dr. Angela Duckworth, she notes there are two types of perseverance: *Uppercase "P" Perseverance and lowercase "p" perseverance. Uppercase "P" Perseverance* is having the fortitude to persevere over a long stretch of time. *Lowercase "p" perseverance* is being able to overcome obstacles and setbacks in the moment. This chapter is all about giving you tools to optimize both versions of perseverance, no matter what you are up against.

Breaking it down another level, think about this. During pressure situations or just everyday life, you are bound to have"ANTs" (Automatic Negative Thoughts) pop-up. To help with in-the-moment recovery, I'm going to teach you how to execute a reset strategy to help get you back to the present—one play, rep, moment, or action at a time. Stack these small wins daily and you'll train that long-term resilience, which is a required skill of any champion.

With the stories I shared in this chapter as your inspiration, can you think of a challenging experience or hardship you have been through or are dealing with now?

Practice reframing this adversity and shifting your perspective to see it as a blessing, not a curse. How can you use this obstacle to help you grow, persevere, have empathy for others, and be a source of personal power?

Our greatest promise lies within our greatest pain. My power source comes from my years of lacking confidence due to insecurities, fear of failure, and bouts with stuttering. Because of those experiences I have a deep sense of empathy for performers of all types and my mission now is to transform lives and normalize mindset training—all because of my struggles. I wouldn't have the drive to do what I do without those challenging experiences. For that I am grateful.

Reset. Refocus. Rise.

Years ago, during a live conference hosted by Johnson & Johnson's Corporate Athlete training for business professionals, I heard the following fact, and it's always stuck with me. According to the Human Performance Institute in Florida, what do you think is the top common trait of number one ranked tennis professionals?

It's not serve velocity or how well they use their backhand. It's being able to recover quickly from failure or adversity. After a mistake, bad call, or unforced error, these top pros have a predetermined routine to center their focus to get back to the present moment. This predetermined routine could look something like this: switching one's racquet to the opposite hand, taking a slow deep breath, finding a spot on the court to recenter one's focus, then getting back into the game.

How quickly do you recover? Take a moment to reflect.

Write down what you currently say to yourself or negative routines you do when you fail or get frustrated:

Do those actions or thoughts help you respond in a positive way and foster a quiet mind?

Temp Check: Get to Green / Find Your Five

As noted earlier, self-awareness is a critical mental skill, especially when managing your mind and body in performance environments. A simple system I teach to maximize your state is knowing your *Internal Temperature* or doing what I call a *"Temp Check."* This is a numeric and 3-color system to identify your physiology, energy, and focus.

Think of a thermometer with vertical numbers listed from bottom to top ranging from 1 through 9. The number one being low and nine being high.

The numbers one, two, and three represent low energy, and a lack of focus and motivation. This is the Blue Zone (think cold or too low). Numbers four, five, and six, represent your sweet spot or sustained peak performance. I call this your Green Zone, which is the ideal spot to be "in the zone" with the right energy and neutral mindset—not too high or too low. Numbers seven, eight, and nine represent an overly heightened arousal state that cannot be sustained and has the potential to sabotage your execution. This is the Red Zone, where you might be "too hot" or your nerves are getting the best of you with a highly elevated heart rate and a loud mind. This is where you've lost control. Here's a visual representation.

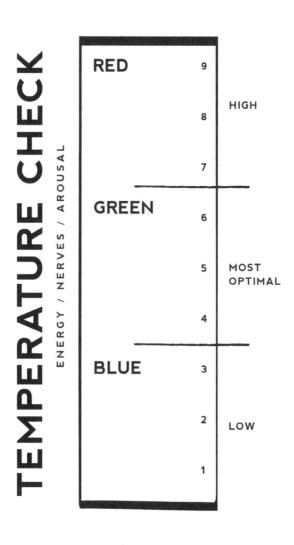

Kind of like the fable of Goldilocks and the Three Bears, one porridge was too cold (Blue), one porridge was too hot (Red), but one porridge was just right (Green). Based on your internal arousal and energy levels, sometimes you need to turn up or turn down the heat. The aim is to *Get to Green or Find Your Five.*

It's important to note that being in red or blue is not always bad. Each moment requires a different zone. When the game or presentation is over, being in a mental place of relaxation and recovery is necessary. That's when being in a "blue" zone and "cooling down" would be good (you'll learn more about recovery in the next chapter). Also, in intense situations, we need to have a heightened boost of adrenaline, energy, and be in the red zone—especially in moments like avoiding being hit by a car or in specific times in combat sports. The skill lies in your awareness and being able to get to the right internal state at the right time. Let's look at a few examples.

Imagine being an Olympic track athlete about to perform in a gold medal relay race. You have trained your whole life for this moment and millions of people across the globe are watching you in that packed arena. If you don't have the tools to stay in control, you will not maximize that opportunity. And if you are in "red" for too long during warm-ups, you will burn precious fuel—mentally and physically. The goal is to do a "temp check" and notice when your internal state is too high or too low. Dial it back down or up with a "reset routine."

The same can be said for business. Before a virtual presentation I often have to check myself and raise my energy to get out of "blue" and into a "green" peak state. Speaking and conducting online trainings at home in my office everyday can sometimes get monotonous. To elevate my energy, I "find my five" by using my body, affirmations, focus keys, and my OPS routine to get the juices flowing.

This quiet mind "temp check" tactic is a perfect compliment to "framing your focus" by controlling what you can control and using routines to get your body, mind, and energy to perform when it matters most.

When I do workshops, I sometimes get the audience to elevate their heart rate through physical activity. For example, I have them do jumping jacks, run in place, or even do burpee's. Then we practice getting our heart rate out of a red zone and down to green through our breath and physical and visual routines.

Coaches and leaders, try this activity. Never in the history of yelling at someone to "calm down," has anyone ever calmed down. We need to allow time to practice how to gain composure and get to green. In moments of preparation and competition, allow your team time to practice being aware of their state—even if it's just pausing for a few seconds to do a *Ten Second Temp Check*. In this moment of self-awareness, take a slow, deep breath and do a quick body scan to identify and adjust when needed.

To help you find your five, here is a system to help when fear, doubt, or negative internal stress spike and you notice you are in the "red." This "green routine" or "reset system" will help you respond like a champion—no matter the circumstances.

Green Routine and Reset Strategy

Below is a quick, three-step system for in-the-moment recovery to get to green.

Step 1 - Reset Word: Come up with a "reset" word or phrase that you will say to yourself to get your thoughts back on track (Examples: *let go . . . breathe . . . I got this*). When you recognize you are feeding the Bad Wolf due to failure, fear, or are in a blue or red zone, say this word or phrase to stop that unproductive thought pattern. Purpose Coach, best-selling author, and influencer, Jay Shetty, calls this process to **Spot, Stop, and Swap** your thoughts. I call it having a **Mindset M.A.P.** with your self-talk—just like a computer operating system looking for viruses in the software.

- M - Monitor your thoughts
- A - Audit out negative or unproductive thoughts or language
- P - Program (or re-program) your brain with productive self-talk

This is a phenomenal tool to help quiet the noise.

Write your reset word/phrase here:

Step 2 - Reset Routine: Develop a quick physical routine (five seconds or less) that you can execute using your body to get back in rhythm (example: take a slow deep breath, redo the straps on your gloves, fix your ponytail, stand up from your desk, adjust your tie, clap your hands, etc.). *Use motion to change your emotion* and get your body into a green state.

Write your physical reset routine here:

Step 3 - Focal Point: Take a slow deep breath and pick a focal point on the field of competition or stage, on a piece of equipment, or in your work environment that will help refocus your attention (some ideas: find the "O" in "HOME" from the scoreboard, look at the American Flag, a clock on the wall; touch a garment of clothing, stare at the water cooler, look at a dot on the top of your shoes, glance at the framed picture of your family on your desk). Exhale fear into that focal point, inhale courage, and feel a sense of calm take over. My reset visual cue are the numbers 2437 on my left arm (Kobe + Steve Gleason's numbers).

List your physical focal point here:

Again, in a team environment as a coach or leader, you would use the language "find your five," and "frame your focus," while showing the number five with your hands and then using your hands on the outside of your eyes to represent blinders. These verbal and visual cues are very helpful for you and your team to stay poised, neutral, calm, and to be the eye of the hurricane... especially when you notice they are in a red or blue zone.

Columbia University performance psychologist Heidi Grant calls this recovery strategy an "if-then plan," which she says increases goal attainment by 300%... yes, 300! Not having a plan is planning to fail. We cannot control events or outcomes, but we can control our response.

Use this space to identify common stress triggers (that's the "if"). After each IF, write down your THEN, as in, your plan to respond.

Here's are two examples:

Business:
IF *I receive a negative email from a customer or co-worker and feel I'm in the "red,"* **THEN** *I'll get up out of my seat and take a few minutes to get a glass of water, gather myself, and respond in a productive way (instead of answering back quickly out of frustration and resentment).*

Sport:
IF *I walk a string of batters or the umpire makes a bad call and I notice I'm moving into "red,"* **THEN** *I'll remove myself from the pitcher's mound, get off the dirt, and execute my "reset routine:"*
- Rub the ball down
- Take a few deep breaths and look at the left field foul pole and say my reset word—"compete"
- Get back on the mound and swipe off the dirt on the rubber to flush the last moment
- Get my sign and attack the next pitch

Now it's your turn. Write down at least three IF-THEN statements below that address moments or situations that cause you to feel acute stress (in "red") and how you will respond with poise and clarity.

IF | THEN

On this topic of resilience, composure, and getting to "green," there is an equation that was originated by success speaker and original author of *Chicken Soup for the Soul,* Jack Canfield. This equation is also a key philosophy taught by leadership consultants, Tim and Brian Kight, who have worked with teams like Ohio State Football and companies around the country. It's this:

$$E + R = O$$
As in, **Event + Response = Outcome.**

In the performance coaching space, this equation is shared often. Here's why, **100% of outcomes in our life are only 10% of events we experience, but 90% on how we choose to respond.** Here is a visual of that breakdown:

Event (10%) + Response (90%) = Outcome (100%)

It's not a matter of if challenges will arise, but **when.**

Adversity is inevitable. Have a plan to use challenges as your golden ticket to find your best. Sailors cannot improve their skills sailing in smooth waters. Unlocking your power falls into a similar position. Adversity, challenge, and change are your greatest opportunities to improve, advance, and rise above the rest.

Holocaust survivor, author, and psychiatrist, Viktor Frankl, once wisely said, "Between stimulus and response there is a space. In that space is our power to choose our response. In our response lies our growth and our freedom."

Wow. Powerful.

Remember, we are conditioning a quiet mind. Don't miss this crucial perspective to stay in control and maximize your performance.

Addition by Subtraction

Up to this point, I've provided you with many tools, techniques, and systems to help you execute and perform at your best. This next strategy is a little different. According to Trevor Moawad, "When you study successful performers, it's not just what they do. It's what they don't do."

The aim is to practice what longtime Major League Baseball Manager, Joe Maddon says, "Do simple better." Identify negative patterns, habits, language, or influences in your life and eliminate them. Removing one to three of these negative factors just might be a simpler approach for you to create and sustain success.

How can you "reset" and apply this addition by subtraction principle? Select three negative habits or influences you will eliminate:

1.

2.

3.

With simplicity comes focus and fewer distractions on your path to success. Yet, there is a barrier to entry for a reason. Always remember to fail forward, learn, and keep going. Failure is a building block toward success. As we move one step closer to the completion of this playbook, it's absolutely vital to learn about the impact of two additional superpowers—reflection and recovery. These two factors cannot be overlooked in one's quest to train a quiet mind.

PLAY IX
RECOVERY AND REFLECTION

Have you ever heard of the name *Sir Roger Bannister?* If you haven't, I'm excited to tell you about this remarkable individual and what it says about human potential. Bannister ran the first sub-four-minute mile in history. This achievement is so remarkable, because for most of human history, scientists and track experts believed the human body was not capable of breaking the four-minute mile barrier. Roger believed he could do it, and once he did, dozens of runners broke that same barrier in just a few years.

To help him achieve this limit shattering accomplishment in human per-formance, Bannister added a unique strategy to his preparation. Running a sub four-minute mile has been achieved many times since 1954, but I would wager that most athletes training to break a record do not take a three-day break just before their big race to go hiking. Yup, that's right—hiking. That's exactly what Bannister did.

He said he felt a bit "stale" and even though he admitted it was "bordering on the lunatic," he also knew he needed to do something different to break out of his rut. He was training to break a record, after all. Can you imagine that type of pressure? Bannister noted that removing himself from his normal elements, connecting with nature, and allowing his mind, body, and soul to recover, was one of the most essential steps he took to break the record. That time away from his regular training regimen allowed Bannister to reflect and receive a mental and physical break. His three-day hike helped him feel refreshed and energized.

What we can learn from this example is that Bannister's secret sauce to track and field immortality was a unique approach to recovery and reflection.

Like Bannister pioneered, we are seeing recovery take a larger focus in the performance world today. For three-time NBA Champion, LeBron James, he says the number one key to his success is sleep. He likes to keep his room at a particular temperature, turn off all electronics—though he sometimes uses the Calm app, which he has recorded a whole series on the importance of sleep—and completely focuses on routines designed to get eight or nine hours of sleep. James notes how recovery not only helps him physically, but emotionally and mentally, too.

"I just think that's just the best way to recover," James said on the Tim Ferriss Show podcast. "I mean, I can do all the training, I can do all the ice bags and the NormaTecs and everything that we do that we have as far as our recovery package while I'm up, but when you get that good sleep, you just wake up and you feel fresh. You don't need an alarm clock. You just feel like 'OK, I can tackle this day at the highest level.'"

In this chapter I'm going to encourage you to harness the power of recovery. As in, take time to process your day and learnings, while prioritizing rest and sleep.

Recovery is the Secret Sauce

"If you told an athlete you had a treatment that would reduce the chemicals associated with stress, that would naturally increase human growth hormone, that enhances recovery rate, that improves performance, they would all do it. Sleep does all of those things."

— Casey Smith, Director of Player Health & Performance, Dallas Mavericks, NBA

"SLEEP IS THE SECRET SAUCE"

— SHAWN STEVENSON, AUTHOR OF SLEEP SMARTER

What is your recovery plan? If a computer has dozens of tabs open or hasn't restarted or shut down for a long time, it will perform slowly and be less effective. The mind is the same way. To re-enter a flow state, one must remove themselves from the activity to recalibrate and recharge. We can't be "on" all the time (hence the Bannister and LeBron examples).

The most effective way we can recover is through quality sleep.

Did you know that when you sleep, your body produces amazing performance enhancers like human growth hormone (HGH) and testosterone? Proper sleep has been proven to improve reaction times, problem solving, speed, accuracy, health, and reduce injury.

Who doesn't want more of that?

Research from sleep expert and author of *Power Sleep*, Dr. James Maas, shows that teenagers require at least 9.15 hours of sleep. Adults need at least seven to eight hours of sleep. And athletes and performers, definitely need at least eight or more hours of good sleep. Performance psychologist Michael Gervais has shared multiple times on his podcast, *Finding Mastery*, that getting only five hours of sleep, five days in a row, has the same negative impact on cognitive and motor skills as driving a car drunk. Yikes! If you aren't prioritizing proper recovery, you simply don't fully care about yourself and the fundamentals of high performance.

Knowing this, while working with clients of all types, I remind them of the **Peak Performance Triad**—as in, there are three phases that make-up one's time and energy as a performer:
1. Training
1. Performing
1. Recovering

My guess is that if you are like most people, you only have a clear plan for one or two of these three phases and you miss a huge opportunity to improve your effectiveness through championship recovery.

If you follow the ultimate GOAT and 7-time Super Bowl Champion, Tom Brady, on Instagram or read his book, *The TB12 Method: How to Achieve a Lifetime of Sustained Peak Performance,* the majority of his content centers around essential recovery strategies—not just about grinding. He shares an abundance of information about muscle pliability, hydration, nutrition, supplements, mindset, rest, and sleep.

With Brady being the first and only 43-year old Super Bowl Champion, not only did he defeat the Kansas City Chiefs in Tampa Bay with millions of people watching worldwide, but he also beat Mother-Nature and Father-Time. Keeping this all-time GOAT super-human accomplishment in mind, I'm definitely paying attention to these recovery strategies. Are you?

Making elite recovery a priority like Brady, it's time to prioritize your rejuvenation habits. Think about consistent healthy routines you will execute post-performance or during the work week that will help you recharge properly.

What will you do immediately after you perform to help with reflection or recovery?

Your post-performance plan:

You already worked on your morning routine, but your nighttime routine is just as important.

What is your bedtime routine?

My favorite reminders to help my clients with a solid bedtime routine are these four keys:

1. Stop watching a screen or phone 30 minutes before you attempt to fall asleep (this minimized blue light exposure and melatonin suppression)

2. Charge your phone away from your bed (I'm guessing if you are like me and your cell phone is close to you at night, you'll be scrolling on social media wee hours into the night. Eliminate this temptation. Will-power is not strong enough!)

3. Try to go to bed around the same time with a consistent "wind-down" routine (examples: read a book, meditate, journal, etc.)

4. Have a glass of water ready to go on your night stand, so when you wake up you can hydrate right away. Why is this important? Here's why: when you wake up, your body hasn't consumed water for around eight hours, so this helps avoid dehydration.

Continue your hydration and fuel plan below.

Proper hydration and fuel plan:

Now onto self-care. Think about nice things you can do to recharge your batteries, partake in other passions, and give yourself energy.

Your weekly self-care goals:

At the highest level, everyone is grinding. That's a given. A powerful way to separate yourself from the competition is in this critical niche of recovery. Master the skill that Michael Jordan's longtime mindset coach and author of *The Mindful Athlete*, George Mumford, calls "right effort." Right effort is putting your time and energy into activities that serve you and are productive rather than unproductive activities that drain you or waste time. I'm sure you can think of a time or two when you were browsing the internet or scrolling through social media and looked up to see you'd wasted an hour of your life. Or you were busy doing non essential tasks that were disguised as work, but you were actually just filling time.

Breaks Are Important

I'm not saying you should strictly focus on tasks that are productive. Everyone needs a break. It's critical to get outside, take a walk or a hike, or just let your mind wander. A *Psychology Today* article written by Meg Selig highlights recent research on the importance of taking productive breaks, including the following findings (cited directly from the article):

- "Movement breaks" are essential to your physical and emotional health.
- Breaks can prevent "decision fatigue."
- Breaks restore motivation, especially for long-term goals.
- Breaks increase productivity and creativity.
- "Waking rest" helps consolidate memories and improve learning.

When will you schedule and encorporate intentional breaks in your day? What will you do to recover during these mini breaks?

My Recovery/Reflection Process

To ball out like Bannister, Beyoncé, or Bezos, or LeBron, it is critical to rest and restore your body and mind.

Now that we talked about the power of sleep, let's talk about the power of optimizing learning and growth through reflection.

I didn't always focus on these keys. My first medical sales job brought me to a breaking point because I was no longer feeling the joy and fulfillment I had when I started in that field. I certainly wasn't resting, recovering, or reflecting. I was just straight grinding. While I was in the middle of my burnout, I looked for an outlet. I found it through mentorship and absorbing as much personal development content as possible, then blogging about my findings. The foundation of my career as a mental conditioning coach is based on learning and reflection.

I started reflecting on the books, podcasts, workshops, and other forms of learning that my mentors provided me and I found on my own. I began to journal, diagram, and break down my newfound knowledge. I expressed my new sense of self-awareness through my writing. I just felt like the stuff I was learning was so applicable to many aspects of my life, and I wanted to share this knowledge with other people who might feel the same.

Now I'm in the business of teaching this process to other people. I like to say "learn, reflect, create." It's in the creation phase where you learn it all over again as you share it with others. Just don't lose the lessons—put your findings out there (blog, podcast, vlog, draw, mentor someone, etc.). Even if you don't want to share your reflections with other people, if you keep a journal or a running list on the Notes app on your phone, you'll have a physical chronicle of the content you've consumed and how it's potentially transformed you.

Some people consume self-help content as a form of entertainment, but never apply the learning. Why consume life-changing information if you don't take notes, summarize the key points that spoke to you, and make changes in your life?

My learning and reflection routine often happens in the morning. Most days I get up, run, and do body lifts all before our five kids wake up. During this time of physical sweat, I also get my mental sweat on by listening to audiobooks, podcasts, or YouTube videos. After each physical workout, I continue my mental workout by jotting down my key learnings from the content I consumed that morning. This process is summed up by the adage:

Don't just think it, ink it. What you don't use, you lose.

Do you have a process to summarize and document new learnings? If not, what will that process be?

Maybe consuming a high number of books isn't your thing. If so, you can practice mindfulness and observe your thoughts and intuition. Your mind is like Google. Ask your subconscious a question, sit in stillness, and simply see what your internal search engine comes up with. It's no surprise you might get clarity, ideas, and omens in the shower, going on a drive in your car, doing dishes, or walking outside. You have great wisdom within if you let yourself quiet your mind and reflect.

Try this: Once your practice, performance, or work day is over, take time to reflect on the day. It's not just my personal experience, but research shows that the most powerful form of learning happens more on reflection than in the moment. Also, writing down your thoughts is a form of mindfulness and helps with memory retention and habit change.

This type of *Quiet Mind* reflection centers around three questions (thanks for the inspiration Brian Cain). It's called GOOD/BETTER/NEXT:

1.   What did you do well? (Good)

2. What are some ways you can improve? (Better)
3. What will you do to address an area of improvement? (Next)

Answer these three prompts in a journal or notebook once your day is over or at the end of each week (this will take just a few minutes).

When and where will you get your GOOD/BETTER/NEXT reps in?

GOOD
BETTER
NEXT

WHAT DID I DO WELL?
WHAT CAN I IMPROVE?
WHAT WILL I DO NEXT?

I encourage you to consistently reflect on yourself and/or check-in with someone you trust. Here is a simple truth: Winners do what non-winners are not willing to do. There is no downside to this exercise, only an upside.

Do what Kobe Bryant called "self-editing." Be honest with yourself. This type of reflective work takes vulnerability and openness, and as you might recall, these are the two cornerstones of peak performance.

The long-term effects of using this practice are huge. Using reflective mindfulness and journaling for weeks, months, or maybe even years, you will have an archive and detailed history of your mindset, growth, and performance (both at times of success and struggle). **This self-scouting has the potential to create the most powerful mental skill of all, self-awareness, and shrink the time you are in a slump.** You can review these entries when needed to understand, duplicate, and scale your success.

Anyone can have success for the short term, but not necessarily the long term. Prioritizing rest, reflection, and recovery will give you the slight edge and will eventually compound into sustained peak performance.

PLAY X
BECOME LIMITLESS

Way to go! Just one more play to master along your journey of discovery and unlocking your inner-greatness. If you are reading this, you have proven to yourself that you are not just interested, but committed to developing a quiet mind.

As I briefly mentioned in the last chapter, a crucial factor that changed my life—and one I hope you implement also—is continuing to stay curious in understanding the power of the mind, learning the fundamentals of success, and investing in your personal development daily. When you do this, you'll elevate your self-image and expand what is possible for you.

Investing In You

Legendary peak performance speaker Jim Rhon once said, "Your level of success will seldom exceed your level of personal development."

With smartphones and the internet, access to information is more readily available than ever before. Ignorance is truly a choice with the tools that are at our disposal:

- Podcasts

- Audiobooks
- YouTube
- E-books
- Google
- Educational videos
- Facebook groups
- Online courses
- Live workshops
- One-on-one and group coaching
- Videos of yourself performing

If you are in school or just finished your degree, your learning shouldn't stop. The average CEO reads about five books a month whereas the average American consumes about three books a year. Is that a coincidence? I think not. What if you read 10 pages or listened to 15 minutes of an audiobook each day? You would easily finish at least one book a month.

What about your commute or chores around the house? What if you listened to 20 minutes of a podcast each day? Imagine the knowledge, best practices, and success stories and strategies you could obtain. Quick tip: Increase the listening speed to 1.25 or 2.0 on your podcasts and audiobooks and consume the content even faster!

I promise, no one lies on their deathbed and says, "Man, I wish I would have watched more Netflix or scrolled more on Instagram while I was alive and healthy."

Oh, heck-to-the-no!

Think of how many hours and days you waste. The world is at your fingertips. The best investment you can make is in yourself. You can learn and become anything. It's time to get your mental sweat on just like getting your physical sweat on.

What is one part of your life or craft in which you would like to innovate or master?

What learning tools do you commit to utilize more to help grow your skills (podcasts, audiobooks, thought leaders on YouTube, videos of yourself executing your craft, etc.)?

Another powerful tool that is often overlooked in helping you become limitless is to seek out mentors. **Success leaves clues.** Who has what you want? Study them (virtual mentors) and connect with them (in-person mentors). We gain wisdom in one of two ways: by experience or by learning from others. Which one is more efficient? I definitely see the value of getting experience, but you will learn and grow much faster by learning from someone who has already been there, done that. There is expensive wisdom (failing yourself) and inexpensive wisdom (learning from the success or failure of others).

Acclaimed entertainer Michael Jackson studied James Brown. Hall of Fame tight-end Tony Gonzalez studied one of the NFL's most prolific receivers, Jerry Rice. Elon Musk studied Albert Einstein (among others). Tony Robbins studied and learned under Jim Rhon. I've studied thousands of hours of content from applied mental experts Brian Cain, Trevor Moawad, Michael Gervais, Tony Robbins, Nicole Lauren Johnson, Graham Betchart, Mel Robbins, Jon Gordon, Lindsey Wilson, Ken Ravizza, Lou Tice, and Brené Brown.

We become and act like who we study and deeply observe because we have what are called "mirror neurons" in our brain—we model and mirror what we see. One of the reasons I created my podcast "Master Your Mindset" is so I could learn from amazing thought leaders like I just listed.

My favorite formula to create content is to get inspired by these thought leaders, then act like a DJ and remix the content by expanding, modifying, and making my own models to understand and teach the mental game.

How do you expand and grow your philosophy? Who or what are you studying? Random dog and cat videos on TikTok? Every series of The Real Housewives on Bravo? If you are not an Esport Athlete, is playing five hours a day on your Xbox the best use of your time? These examples though cute, funny, crazy, and/or entertaining—probably won't give you the same return as studying someone who is killing it in your craft.

A person who has what you want and whom you can learn from is:

You will ask them to be your mentor by this date:

List others who can help you grow your skills and expand your success. Include when and how you will connect with them:

List mentors you will study online or through podcasts and books:

Knowledge

To help you on your journey of personal development and self-discovery, check out some of my favorite books, podcasts, and performance experts:

BOOKS

- *Greenlights*, Matthew McConaughey
- *Atomic Habits: An Easy & Proven Way to Build Good Habits and Break Bad Ones*, James Clear
- *Peak Performance: Elevate Your Game, Avoid Burnout, and Thrive with the New Science of Success*, Brad Stulberg, Brad Magness
- *Stillness is the Key: An Ancient Strategy to Modern Life*, Ryan Holiday
- *Think and Grow Rich*, Napoleon Hill
- *The Happiness Advantage: How a Positive Brain Fuels Success in Work and Life*, Shawn Achor
- *The Inner Game of Tennis: The Classic Guide to the Mental Side of Peak Performance*, W. Timothy Gallwey
- *The Power of Positive Leadership: How and Why Positive Leaders Transform Teams and Organizations and Change the World*, Jon Gordon
- *The Subtle Art of Not Giving a F*ck: A Counterintuitive Approach to Living a Good Life*, Mark Manson
- *It Takes What It Takes*, Trevor Moawad
- *The Source: The Secrets of the Universe, the Science of the Brain*, Tara Swart
- *Innercise: The New Science to Unlock Your Brain's Power*, John Assaraf
- *The Slight Edge: Turning Simple Disciplines into Massive Success and Happiness*, Jeff Olson and John David Mann
- *Influence: The Psychology of Persuasion*, Robert B. Cialdini
- *The Greatest Salesman in the World*, Og Mandino
- *Mind Gym: An Athlete's Guide to Inner Excellence*, Gary Mack and David Casstevens
- *The Secret*, Rhonda Byrne

PODCASTS

- Master Your Mindset: Tools to Win the Inner-Game, Collin Henderson
- Room Tilters by Limitless Minds
- High Performance Mindset with Dr. Cindra Kamphoff
- The Brian Cain Mental Performance Podcast
- The Science of Success, Matt Bodnar
- Impact Theory with Tom Bilyeu
- Finding Mastery, Michael Gervais
- The School of Greatness, Lewis Howes
- The Ed Mylett Show
- How I Built This with Guy Raz (NPR)

THOUGHT LEADERS

- Brian Cain
- Steven Kotler
- Tom Bilyeu
- Dr. Sasha Heinz
- Dr. Michael Gervais
- Dr. Joe Dispenza
- Tony Robbins
- Hanna Huesman
- Graham Betchart
- Dr. Cindra Kamphoff
- Dr. Andrew Huberman
- Dr. Susan David
- Lindsey Wilson
- Jon Gordon
- Jim Kwik
- Dr. Brené Brown
- Ed Mylett
- Trevor Moawad
- Mel Robbins
- Justin Su'a
- Lauren Nicole Johnson

There's just too many to list!!! Look these game changers up on social media and YouTube to transform your mind!

Self-Image

By studying the content from titans in your field, you will generate the insights necessary to unlock your true potential. By applying these learnings, this act will naturally upgrade your behaviors and how you see yourself. This process of identity-shaping is also called your **self-image**. Elevating your self-image is a powerful, proven strategy when it comes to investing in yourself and becoming limitless. The most powerful force is how you see yourself. Your limits begin where your vision ends.

I first learned the importance of self-image from the best-selling book *Psycho Cybernetics*, by Dr. Maxwell Maltz. Originally written in 1960, this book is considered a cognitive behavioral training classic and groundbreaking in the field of mental performance and well-being. When I first heard the book title I was a little confused. What does *"Psycho Cybernetics"* even mean? In this case, "psycho," means *relating to the mind or psychology*. "Cybernetics," translated in Greek means, *to steer your ship to port*. Put these concepts together, and as Maltz once explained, the aim is "steering your mind to a productive, useful goal so you can reach the greatest port in the world... peace of mind."

Dr. Maltz uncovered this realization in his career as a plastic surgeon. While working in this field he found that while many patients loved their new look, a number of patients would not improve their confidence and self-esteem after surgery.

Why was this?

Over time, Maltz discovered that the patient's perception (whether good or bad) came down to one simple factor: the internal image the person held within themself. He found that just by getting his patients to change their self-image through self-affirmations and visualization techniques, they experienced much better post-surgery outcomes. What's astonishing is that by doing this mental work with his patients, some of them no longer felt the need for surgery. This concentration on inner attitudes was essential to his approach. As he discovered: **a person's outer success can never rise above the one visualized internally.**

His work showed that the primary factor of whether or not a person succeeds or fails, or finds happiness or sadness, is often directly tied to how they see themself. There are so many fantastic quotes from Dr. Maltz and his experience understanding the power of self-image. Here are a few of my favorites.

"You will act like the sort of person you conceive yourself to be."

"If you make friends with yourself you will never be alone."

"Self-image sets the boundaries of individual accomplishment."

"Our self-image and our habits tend to go together. Change one and you will automatically change the other."

"Low self-esteem is like driving through life with your hand-brake on."

"Your most important sale in life is to sell yourself to yourself."

So good, right? If you can upgrade your self-image, you will improve your:
- Relationships
- Health
- Well-being
- Fulfillment
- Performance

Now let's examine how you can improve your self-image. Here are some tactics.

Self-Love + Energy

Most people spend the majority of their time obsessing over their flaws and coming up with reasons why they can't do something. One of the biggest shifts I had to make to improve my mindset was stopping old limiting beliefs by having self-compassion—especially around speaking in public and needing validation. Once I began to practice "radical self acceptance" (RSA), I saw a direct correlation in the improvement of my well-being, which in turn helped my fluency improve. I remember thinking to myself, If I stutter, so what. *No one ever speaks perfectly. I have many traits to be proud of. Just be myself... that is enough.*

Shifting my focus to who I was, instead of who I wasn't, was a huge factor in my growth and happiness.

Key question: *Do you love yourself unconditionally? Do you play to your strengths or get bogged down by one or two shortcomings?* In order to change your outer world, you must change your inner world first. Try this: When you look in the mirror, look for the good, instead of just seeing what you don't like. Learn to love those parts too. That's what makes you different, and that is what makes you awesome. I often tell the people I coach to master this phrase: *"I love what I have".*

As Dr. Maltz once said, "The most delightful surprise in life is to suddenly recognize your own worth."

Here is a vital mental realignment to see who you truly are: **Stop wasting your energy reviewing all the things you don't have.** Instead, focus on your strengths and **double down on what you do have.** This is an important progression in growing your inner picture. Through this healthy self-image lense, what activities play to your strengths?

Philosopher, theologian, and civil rights leader Howard Thurman once said, "Don't ask yourself what the world needs. Ask yourself what makes you come alive and go do that, because what the world needs is people who have come alive."

Here is a way to find your best self. Examine these questions.

What lights you up and gives you energy? What comes easily to you? What makes you unique and different? Do more of that and watch your identity and performance take off!

Scratch an itch, find a niche, and you'll be rich.

Not sure what that activity or topic is for you? Try this. Find your *deepest curiosity* and you will find unlimited energy. What do you research? What do you talk about? What topics or areas of interest fill your mind endlessly? This is a crucial step in cracking the code to unlock your best.

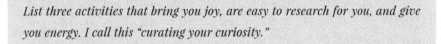

List three activities that bring you joy, are easy to research for you, and give you energy. I call this "curating your curiosity."

1.

2.

3.

How can you do more of what you just listed—especially in your role, job, or sport? I love this concept: *Find your uniqueness and exploit it in the service of others.*

This is a fantastic tactic to leverage what you have and put yourself in positions of curiosity to drive success. Maybe you can make this area of expertise a side hustle that can turn into a main hustle. That's what I did.

Future Self

Another tool to improve your self-image involves writing down several "best version of me" statements. There are three yous: the real, ideal, and public self. Which one do you focus on?

Don't find yourself, create yourself. **When you identify the person you would like to be or the success you desire, write it down as if you already are that person or have those things.** Repeat these statements to yourself daily.

When you write and speak an "I am" and/or "I have" statement (even if you do not have it yet), you are commanding your subconscious to be and attract those characteristics and achievements.

Some examples:

I am a finisher.

I am compassionate.

I do what I say I'm going to do.

I am present.

I have health.

I have wealth.

I have unshakable confidence.

I am a New York Times best-selling author.

I have wonderful and fulfilling relationships.

I am an all-star athlete.

I have a seven-figure business.

I've experienced this phenomenon firsthand. When we moved several years ago I found an old journal where I set professional and financial goals for myself covering a five year span. When I revisited these affirming goals (which I had forgotten I even wrote down), I was within $3K each year from what I journaled and I had finally attained the career I dreamed of. I showed Kendra this list almost in tears. Thoughts really do become things after all. Are you using this fundamental law of success?

Now it's your turn. Be as specific as you can. Set a reminder on your phone to see these statements as the "best version of you" daily. Read and say them aloud at least twice a day. What you will find is that these traits will begin to feel normal and you will act in accordance with your internal commands.

Write down several "best version of you" statements here:

Why is this exercise so important? Here's why: We act as we see ourselves to be. According to the author of *Atomic Habits*, James Clear, our identity is the number one driver of our habits and behaviors.

You can add another layer to make your "best version of you" statements even stronger. Here's how: To be credible with yourself, list accomplishments, actions, or habits you have performed that back up these affirmations. This form of internal credibility will support these identity statements. For example, if you wrote down you are a hard worker, list what you've done to support this.

List actions and habits below that support your "best version of you" statements. Said differently, what have you been doing to establish internal credibility through doing difficult things, executing success habits, and putting in the work?

This technique is used by best-selling author, former Navy SEAL, and former pull-ups world record holder, David Goggins. He calls this type of self-talk his "cookie jar." When he is feeling doubt or faced with adversity, he quickly thinks about times when he has overcome challenges and shifts his focus to these "cookie jar" moments. Goggins, who now competes in ultra-marathons, reflects and stores these memories when he needs them. This gives him the power to keep fighting and endure.

Do you have a mental cookie jar?

Self-Image Comfort Zone

Stress occurs when you perform differently from your ideal picture of yourself. This phenomenon is just like a thermostat. What does that mean? Well, if the temperature of a room is set at 68 degrees and it gets cold (say 60 degrees), the heat will kick on to get the temperature back up. If the room gets too hot (say 80 degrees), the air conditioner will turn on to get the temperature back down. Our self-image comfort zone operates the same way.

YOU'LL NEVER OUTPERFORM YOUR SELF-IMAGE

We feel stress when we are under-performing and work hard to get back to where we see ourselves. We feel just as much stress when we are over-performing and often sabotage our performances and fall back to our comfort zone.

Let's use softball as a simple example. Inspired by the book *Baseball's 6th Tool*, author John D. Curtis explains this self-image comfort zone phenomenon. If a softball hitter sees herself as a .275 hitter but starts the season hitting .200, she will feel stressed and work like heck to get back up to around .270–.280. However, if her batting average jumps up to around .340, she will feel just as much stress trying to maintain that level of success and expectation. Because this player doesn't completely believe in herself and has imposter syndrome, she will find a way to fail, sabotage her performance, and get back down to her .275 comfort zone.

This same principle can be applied to money, sales numbers, business, health, and relationships. Being uncomfortable and fearing success is very similar to being uncomfortable and fearing failure.

What is your self-image comfort zone?

For me, my only goal was to get a college athletic scholarship. I did not see myself beyond that image. And guess what, that is where my career finished.

You must constantly work on this and raise your self-image thermostat by setting stretch goals, visualizing success daily, identifying and performing the behaviors of champions, and upgrading your self-talk—not just for one day or week, but all the time!

When you fail, say, "That's not like me."

When you succeed, say, "That's like me."

Forget your failures, but remember the lessons.

Another key factor of improving your self-image comfort zone is who you surround yourself with.

To steal from Academy Award-winning actor Denzel Washington:
If you hang around five confident people, you'll be the sixth. If you hang around five intelligent people, you'll be the sixth. If you hang around five millionaires, you'll be the sixth. If you hang around five idiots, you'll be the sixth.

This concept speaks to me:

Show me your friends and I'll show you your habits.

Show me your habits and I'll show you your future.

Take a moment right now and reflect on who you are spending most of your time with. Their words and actions are most likely rubbing off on you. It might be time to make a few adjustments. Also, reflect on the type of energy you are taking or making based off of your mindset and commitment to excellence. Is it time to upgrade the energy you are putting out?

YOU BECOME WHO YOU SURROUND YOURSELF WITH

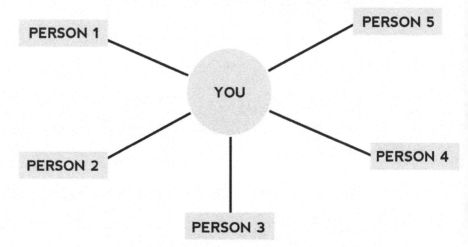

CHOOSE WISELY

I hope this book is helping you rise to your full potential, thus bringing more value to those around you. Never forget: Like attracts like. Your vibe attracts your tribe.

Once you alter the picture of yourself by upgrading your thoughts, habits, and who you surround yourself with, you will change and grow toward your new picture.

How can you become what you don't see, practice, or believe? Upgrade your beliefs, standards, and behaviors, and like a tide, your performance will rise.

These are the laws of success. Never stop investing in you and your vision.

MENTAL COOLDOWN
IT'S GO TIME

Did you know that only 10% of people who consume self-books get past the first chapter? The fact that you are here is awesome. Great job! You are the exception not the rule. In that vein, this is not the type of book you should only read once. Challenge yourself to come back to these concepts and relearn what you learned often—and definitely every six months or at least once a year. That is what mental conditioning is all about—mastering the fundamentals.

Speaking of fundamentals, take a moment now to do a post Quiet Mind Assessment on several self-awareness areas. Let's see if you've improved from when you started reading this book.

1. Where has your focus been in the past week? Think about these three time frames, and divide your focus into each category, making sure it adds up to 100 percent.

Past ___% Present ___% Future ___%

2. How have your thoughts been? Divide your self-talk into each category, making sure they add up to 100 percent.

Unproductive Self-Talk (Bad Wolf or negative thinking) ___%

Productive Self-Talk (Good Wolf or neutral to positive thoughts) ___%

Did you notice improvements with your focus and self-talk?

3. How often are you getting your mental reps in? This can include journaling, mindfulness, utilizing the HAW and OPS visualization systems, breathing techniques, practicing productive self-talk, reflecting with Good/Better/Next, stretching your comfort zones, being of service to others, practicing gratitude, executing your process and "reset" routines, and investing in your personal development from books, podcasts, coaches, and mentors.

Rate yourself below on a scale from 1 - 10 (1-low and 10-high) on how much time you have been training a Quiet Mind:

Low - 1 2 3 4 5 6 7 8 9 10 - High

Where have you seen improvements with your mental game?

What tool or strategy has been the most impactful?

What tactic or area do you need to do more of or focus on improving?

Check back and see how you've improved from your mindset baseline from chapter one (Play I: Self-Awareness). Being intentional with your focus, self-talk, and getting your mental reps in are three critical areas that will help elevate your performance. There are no finish lines. Excellence is a lifestyle, not a destination. Never stop going to the mind gym.

Here is one of my favorite quotes from entrepreneur extraordinar and best-selling author of Living with a Seal, Jesse Itzler,

"You didn't come this far to just come this far."

Think about this motivational quote as you continue your journey of inner-peace. Side note: Itzler is also married to Sara Blakely... talk about a dynamic duo! Both are great follows on Instagram, check them out

As you've learned from this book and through personal experiences, nothing worthwhile is ever easy. There is a barrier to greatness for a reason. And that's the best part. If it were easy, everyone would do it. Don't forget this!

Bamboo Baller

Success is like the bamboo tree. When it is planted, nothing happens above ground for many years. This doesn't mean it's not growing, though. All the growth is happening underground. The roots are growing bigger and deeper each day. Then, after about five years, the bamboo tree grows an astonishing 80 feet in six weeks!

I call this being a "bamboo baller." Like the bamboo, be patient. Keep showing up. Trust the process, and great things will come.

You might not see rapid results instantly, but like any new skill—building muscle, endurance, or confidence—it takes repetition after repetition until it becomes instinct. It's the aggregation of marginal gains. Once you've repped these daily habits long enough, I believe you will see a tipping point or compound effect in which your performance will really take off and improve.

15 Minutes = 1% Better

When you break it down, this mental work is only about 15 minutes each day. That's it! Let's put that into perspective. There's 1,440 minutes in each day. Fifteen minutes is just one percent of that day. Focus on getting 1% better by carving out at least 15 minutes for your mental fitness. It's time to condition your mindset with more productive habits. The tools in this book should be your guide.

I've asked before, but it's worth repeating: How much time do you spend on your craft or technical skills? How often do you condition your body? Or what about social media, YouTube, TV, Netflix, or apps on your phone? Your return on investment will be much greater through investing in your mental health versus comparing yourself to others, seeking external validation, procrastinating, or making excuses.

The Greek philosopher Plato once said, "The first and greatest victory is to conquer yourself." I believe this is so true.

Another quote I want you to focus on is from one of my favorite leaders, Nelson Mandela. He once said, "I never lose, I either win or learn." That's so good!

Remember, failure isn't the opposite of success, but part of the journey. If you falter, get knocked down, or lose confidence, just remember that is part of the process. Keep going. Failure shouldn't be a devastation, but an education.

The time is now for you. The biggest growth potential isn't physical, but mental. You already have the power inside of you. It's time to let your mind get out of the body's way and max out what you were born to do. Trust your training and always remember that your sport, profession, position, or craft does not define you. Your worth to the world is not predicated by outcomes, but by being present, authentic, serving others, and growing daily.

Continue to build your quiet mind, show up daily, and reap the rewards forever.

References & Resources

I've included some of my favorite quotes, as well as citations for many of the studies and/or articles I referenced.

- "The happiness of your life depends on the quality of your thoughts." – Marcus Aurelius
- "Our life is shaped by our mind, for we become what we think." –Buddha
- "Every day of our lives, we are on the verge of making those slight changes that would make all the difference." –Mignon McLaughlin
- "A mind that is stretched by a new experience can never go back to it's old dimension." –Oliver Wendell Holme
- "I believe just as strongly in the importance of mental fitness as I do about physical fitness." –Tom Brady
- "There is nothing either good or bad, but thinking makes it so." –William Shakespeare, from Hamlet
- "Be very careful about what you think. Your thoughts run your life." – Proverbs 4:23
- "What you think others think of you sounds a lot like what you think of you." –Sasha Heinz
- "The cave you fear to enter holds the treasure that you seek." –Joseph Campbell
- "As much as you want to feel good physically, I think the biggest battle is how you feel mentally stepping on the field." –Rose Lavelle
- "If you don't rule your mind, it can rule you." –Eliud Kipchoge
- "Concentration and mental toughness are the margins of victory." –Bill Russell
- "The successful warrior is the average man, with laser-like focus." –Bruce Lee
- "A man is great not because he hasn't failed; a man is great because failure hasn't stopped him." –Confucius
- "It's not about the number of hours you practice, it's about the number of hours your mind is present during the practice." –Kobe Bryant
- "He who is not courageous enough to take risks will accomplish nothing in life." –Muhammad Ali

- "In the middle of difficulty lies opportunity." –Albert Einstein
- "I always visualized my success. The process of seeing success before it happened put me in a positive frame of mind and prepared me to play the game." –Michael Jordan
- "It's the repetition of affirmations that leads to belief. And once that belief becomes a deep conviction, things begin to happen." –Muhammad Ali
- "It's impossible to hit and think at the same time." –Yogi Berra
- "The less effort, the faster and more powerful you will be." –Bruce Lee
- "Mental toughness is really all about not getting too high or getting too low. It's about staying pretty even keel. That's kind of the trick to it, not to get emotionally attached to the situation." –Kobe Bryant
- "They can prepare for a month on what we do, but they cannot prepare for who I know we are." –Dabo Swinney
- "Whatever is in the past has already been done. I'm trying to do the best I can in the here and now. You've got to be present when you play." –Tiger Woods
- "Our words and what we say out loud represent the wardrobe of our beliefs." –Zach Brandon
- "If my mind wasn't in the present moment, the here and now, my body and energy wouldn't be either. The present was something I could control, unlike those useless thoughts about the past or future situation that wasn't in my control at all." –Joe Montana
- "Don't let what you cannot do interfere with what you can do." –John Wooden
- "I would tell players to relax and never think about what's at stake. Just think about the basketball game. If you start to think about who is going to win the championship, you've lost your focus." –Michael Jordan
- "You can make all the excuses you want, but if you're not mentally tough and you're not prepared to play every night, you're not going to win." –Larry Bird
- "The pursuit is happiness." –Graham Betchart
- "While the greats mastered the body, the greatest mastered the mind." –LeBron James

Citations

Aside from the thought leaders, books, and studies I referenced in Quiet Mind, here is an additional list of sources that I either cited directly or that inspired my thought process. Some of the information shared has been absorbed in conferences or through stories I've heard. Regardless, I've made a tremendous effort to give credit where exceptional credit is due.

"21 Benefits of Deep Breathing (Based on Groundbreaking Research!)," Project Monkeymind.com. July 20, 2017
https://www.projectmonkeymind.com/2017/07/benefits-of-deep-breathing/

Blaszczak-Boxe, Agata. "Talking To Yourself Is One Simple Way To Get Better At A New Skill,"
Huffington Post. July 8, 2016.
https://www.huffpost.com/entry/heres-one-simple-way-to-get-better-at-a-new-skill_n_577ffc4be4b0c59of7e95357?guccounter=1&guce_referrer=aHR0cHM6Ly93d3cuZ29vZ2xlLmNvbVS8&guce_referrer_sig=AQA-AAL2pe-sswKWbP1aRTURI8d7pOWinqJvR_LSVqtONedwdMJGuo8ph3Y7kRqa-Of6IB6EOrgCYRbrC_yd7gub1jNOHt6IvGxqizNoli5sqnNSgpS9P5KipDi2uX_8I-b5ry17LiXc6ZW8KUgyvDnWghOzA3orca62sUM9wl3n45q81kA

Brady, T. (2020). The TB12 Method: How to Achieve a Lifetime of Sustained Peak Performance. S.L.: Simon & Schuster.

Burns, D. D. (2002). Feeling Good: The New Mood Therapy. New York: William Morrow.

Canfield, J. (2013). Chicken Soup for the Soul: Readers Choice 20th Anniversary Edition. Simon & Schuster.

Chamine, S. (2016). Positive Intelligence: Why Only 20% of Teams and Individuals Achieve Their True Potential and How You Can Achieve Yours. Austin, TX: Greenleaf Book Group Press.

Clear, J. (2017). Atomic Habits: An Easy & Proven Way to Build Good Habits & Break Bad Ones. Penguin Publishing Group.

Curtain, Melanie. "In an 8-Hour Day, the Average Worker Is Productive for This Many Hours,"
Inc.com. July 21, 2016.
https://www.inc.com/melanie-curtin/in-an-8-hour-day-the-average-worker-is-productive-for-this-many-hours.html

Curtis, J. D. (2012). Baseball's 6th Tool: The Inner Game. La Crosse, Wis.: Coulee Press.

David, S. (2018). Emotional Agility: Get Unstuck, Embrace Change, and Thrive in Work and Life. Penguin USA.

Davis, Scott. "LeBron James has a Detailed Sleep Plan, and His Trainer Says it's the Key to His
'Never-Ending' Recovery," Business Insider. November 28, 2018. https://www.businessinsider.com/lebron-james-says-sleep-critical-recovery-2018-11

Dorfman, H. A. (2016). Coaching the Mental Game: Leadership Philosophies and Strategies for Peak Performance in Sports - and Everyday Life. Taylor Trade Pub.

Duckworth, A. (2017). Grit: Why Passion and Resilience Are the Secrets to Success. London: Vermilion.

Ferriss, Tim. "LeBron James and His Top-Secret Trainer, Mike Mancias (#349)." The Tim Ferriss
Show. Podcast audio, November 27, 2018.
https://tim.blog/2018/11/27/lebron-james-mike-mancias/

Frankl, V. E. (2006). Man's Search for Meaning: An Introduction to Logotherapy. Boston: Beacon Press. (Original work published 1946).

Gonzalez, D. C. (2016). The Art of Mental Training: A Guide to Performance Excellence. North Mankato, Mn: Createspace Independent Publishing Platform.

Gordon, Jon. "Winning and What Truly Matters." Positive University. Podcast audio, July 12,
2019. https://player.fm/series/positive-university-podcast/winning-and-what-truly-
matters-tony-bennett

Grant- Halvorson, H. (2012). Succeed: How We Can Reach Our Goals. New York: Penguin Group.

"Gratitude is Good Medicine," UC Davis Health. November 25, 2015. https://health.ucdavis.edu/medicalcenter/features/2015-2016/11/20151125_gratitude.htm

Hill, N. (2019). Think And Grow Rich. S.L.: Simon & Brown.

Holiday, R. (2019). Stillness is the Key: An Ancient Strategy for Modern Life. London: Profile Books.

"How Many Productive Hours in a Work Day? Just 2 Hours, 23 Minutes..." Vouchercloud.com. https://www.vouchercloud.com/resources/office-worker-productivity

"How the Story Transforms the Teller | Donald Davis | TEDxCharlottesville." Filmed December
23, 2014. YouTube video, 17:33. Posted December 23, 2014. https://www.youtube.com/watch?v=wgeh4xhSA2Q&feature=youtu.be

Ingle, Sean. "Roger Bannister, a Gentleman Who Almost Didn't Run Race that Defined Him,"

The Guardian. March 4, 2018.
https://www.theguardian.com/sport/2018/mar/04/roger-bannister-gentle-man-almost-never-ran-race-defined-him

Itzler, J. (2016). Living with a SEAL: 31 Days Training with the Toughest Man on the Planet. New York: Center Street.

Kotler, S. (2021). The Art of Impossible: A Peak Performance Primer. New York: Harper Wave.

Maas, J. B. (1999). Power Sleep: The Revolutionary Program that Prepares Your Mind for Peak Performance. New York: Quill/Harpercollins.

Mack, G., & Casstevens, D. (2001). Mind Gym: An Athlete's Guide to Inner Excellence. New York, NY: Mcgraw-Hill.

Maltz, M., & Powers, M. (2010). Psycho-Cybernetics: A New Way to Get More Living Out of Life. Chatsworth, CA: Wilshire Book Co.

Manson, M. (2017). The Subtle Art Of Not Giving A F*CK. HarperOne.

Moawad, T. (2020). It Takes What It Takes : How to Manage Negativity, Thrive in Chaos, and Conquer Any Goal. HarperCollins Publishers.

Mumford, G. (2016). The Mindful Athlete: Secrets to Pure Performance. Berkeley, CA: Parallax Press.

Nicklaus, J. and Bowden, K. Golf My Way. New York: Simon & Schuster, 1974.

Pink, D. H. (2012). A Whole New Mind: Why Right-Brainers Will Rule the Future. New York: Riverhead Books.

Pink, D. H. (2018). Drive: The Surprising Truth About What Motivates Us. S.L.: Canongate Books Ltd.

Ravizza, K., & Hanson, T. (2016). Heads-Up Baseball 2.0: 5 Skills for Competing One Pitch at a Time. Tampa, FL: Hanson House.

Selig, Meg. "How Do Work Breaks Help Your Brain? 5 Surprising Answers," Psychology Today.
April 18, 2017. https://www.psychologytoday.com/us/blog/changepower/201704/how-do-work-breaks-help-your-brain-5-surprising-answers

Tewksbury, B. (2020). Ninety Percent Mental: An All-Star Player Turned Mental Skills Coach Reveals the Hidden Game of Baseball. S.L.: Da Capo.

About the Author

Collin Henderson is the founder and CEO of Master Your Mindset, LLC, an industry leader in the field of mental conditioning. He is a speaker, podcast host, and author of six books and two journals focused on peak performance. Collin received both his undergraduate and master's degrees from Washington State University where he was a starting two-sport athlete, a Pac-12 champion, and an academic All-American.

Collin has more than a decade of experience as a sales professional and sales trainer with two Fortune 500 companies in the medical industry, in which he set sales records, won multiple representative of the year honors, and number one finishes.

Since starting his company, Master Your Mindset, Collin's innovative trainings on mindset, culture, and high performance have been utilized by some of the world's best organizations and institutions including: Nike, Zillow, Los Angeles Dodgers Academy, lululemon, Alaska Airlines, Amazon, Microsoft, Salesforce, Stryker, Novartis, GSK, Windermere, FedEx, Paychex, Horizon Pharmaceuticals, US Soccer Foundation, Tulane University, Oregon State University, Seattle University, Northern Arizona University, University of Portland, San Jose State University, and Miami University (and many more).

Collin is a regular mental conditioning contributor to Russell Wilson's groundbreaking company, Limitless Minds, which provides elite mindset training to some of the nation's top corporations including Johnson & Johnson, GE, Goldman Sachs, Harvard Business School, and Chick-fil-A.

Collin and his wife Kendra have five beautiful children and live in Nashville, Tennessee.

For more information on how to master your mindset and build a quiet mind, visit: thecollinhenderson.com

Search "Collin Henderson" or "Master Your Mindset" on Amazon.com, Spotify, or iTunes

Find Collin on Instagram, Facebook, and LinkedIn at @CollinHenderson / His Twitter handle is @c_hen83

You can also check out Collin's other books and journals on Amazon.com:
Project Rise: 8 Winning Habits to Build the Best Version of You
Rise Journal: A Simple Yet Powerful System to Be The Best Version of You Each Day
Master Your Mindset: A Guide to Win the Inner-Game and Unlock the Power of Flow
Flow Journal: A Daily Guide to Master Your Mindset
Positive Parenting: Tools and Tactics to Support Your Child in Competition and Life
Culture is King: 5 Keys to Build a High Performing Team
Culture Toolbox: 40 Team-Building Exercises to Transform Your Culture

Made in USA - Kendallville, IN
72591_9798466610819
05.02.2022 1356